# TACK NOW, SKIPPER

# Owen Parker
# TACK NOW, SKIPPER

ADLARD COLES LIMITED
**GRANADA PUBLISHING**
London Toronto Sydney New York

Published by Granada Publishing in
Adlard Coles Limited, 1979

Granada Publishing Limited
Frogmore, St Albans, Herts AL2 2NF
and
3 Upper James Street, London W1R 4BP
Suite 405, 4th Floor, United Nations Plaza, New York, NY 10017, USA
Q164 Queen Victoria Buildings, Sydney, NSW 2000, Australia
100 Skyway Avenue, Toronto, Ontario, Canada M9W 3A6
PO Box 84165, Greenside, 2034 Johannesburg, South Africa
CML Centre, Queen and Wyndham, Auckland 1, New Zealand

Copyright © Owen Parker 1979

ISBN 0 229 11620 5

Printed and bound in Great Britain at
William Clowes & Sons Limited
Beccles and London

# Contents

# Acknowledgements

When anybody writes a book of this nature, he must have help from many people; this is no exception. I am grateful to Sparkman and Stephens for permission to reproduce the deck plan of the second *Morning Cloud*, and to Ron Holland who has kindly given the same blessing for the boat he has designed. Lewmar Marine have given their permission to use photographs from their library, as have the Australian Information Service, the *Daily Telegraph*, the Press Association, and the *Daily Express*; the *Sunday Express* has allowed me to quote the passage on page 25.

I cannot measure the debt I owe to John and Llewellyn Ryland for being so understanding over the years when it has been a question of time off to sail. Similarly I owe much to the various owners and crews with whom I have raced. You will read in the book my feelings for John Millar, Guy Bowles and Edward Heath so I will not elaborate here, except to thank Mr Heath for reading the typescript and for the kind words he has been good enough to write in his foreword.

Finally I must mention Jeremy Howard-Williams, without whose untiring help the book would not have been possible, and Jack Purdy whose idea it was in the first place.

*Southampton 1979*                                                      *OP*

# Foreword

*by The Rt Hon Edward Heath MBE MP*

What was it like in the old days, what is going on now, what will happen in the future? These questions are not limited to the sailing fraternity; they are ones we all like to ask but which few can answer.

In *Tack now, Skipper*–how often have I heard that cry in the ten years during which he has been a member of the crew of *Morning Cloud*–Owen Parker enlightens us on all three counts.

He draws on his wide experience of boats–ocean racers, twelve metres, six metres, Dragons and other one-designs; of races–the America's Cup, the Admiral's Cup, the Onion Patch, the Southern Cross Cup and the Southern Ocean Racing Conference, the Fastnet, the Bermuda Race and the Sydney–Hobart Race, the Solent Series, Cowes Week, Burnham Week and Ramsgate Regatta; of people with whom he has sailed on seas all over the world. And not content with all this he gives us an insight into the world of marine business as well.

We can delight in his reminiscences of the past, rejoice in his commitment to the present and argue about his forecasts for the future, knowing that there are few people better qualified to hold our interest steadily between the two covers of a book. And as the reader progresses he will come to recognise the authentic voice of Owen Parker, sailing master, tactician, businessman, demanding, cajoling, damning, praising, sparing neither himself, nor the crew nor boat nor business in his determination to win.

We who have sailed with him wish Owen Parker the same success with this book which he has had on the sea. He deserves it.

*20 Sep 78*                                                                 *EH*

# one  Origins

Yachting has given me a wonderful life. I've travelled the world, mixed with barrow boys and barons, pothunters and politicians, and gypsies and gentlemen, and I can honestly say that I have loved every minute of it. When you remember that somebody else has usually been paying, it makes you wonder why anyone should be so lucky.

## Early Days

It all started down on the Itchen Ferry, which is a place so called because of the ferry which used to run between Woolston and Southampton, across the river Itchen, which flows into the top of Southampton Water. The Itchen was where the local yachtsmen and fishermen kept their boats–those who didn't prefer the Hamble River, a little further down on the eastern side of the big inlet. Because Southampton Water is so deep and sheltered (it has four or five fathoms at low water, is nearly ten miles long and lies under the protection of the Isle of Wight immediately to the south of its mouth), it is ideal for big vessels, so Southampton was the home of the trans-Atlantic liners, and there were shipbuilding and repair yards in the vicinity. These, together with the various yacht yards which abounded, afforded good winter work for the men who followed the somewhat precarious existence of the professional yacht racing hand. That's where the Parkers, the Cousins and the Diapers, all well known fishing and sailing families, came from. Traditionally they fished or worked in the shipyards during the winter, and went yacht racing as paid hands in the summer.

My father served his time in the local yard as a shipwright, but only worked at it for a year before following the local tradition. He never made skipper, for he died at the early age of forty-two while playing football. My brother Rennie made skipper before Dad died–he is sometimes with me now in *Morning Cloud* and, though he is older than me, he's very good on board and never tries to tell me what to do. I don't say he doesn't want to sometimes, but he either keeps it to himself, or waits for me to ask for his comments–which I often do, because he has had even more experience of racing in the Solent than I have.

Of course, the old-time professional's life was very much hand to mouth. He seldom knew whether next season's wages were secure, for the owner only had to decide on a smaller boat, or to marry a woman who disliked sailing, and he could be stood off. So I have always been grateful to have a job in the yachting business which has enabled me to take time off when necessary. In my early days, the owners used to pay my business wages while I was sailing with them, as I thought it was unfair to expect my firm to pay for my leisure. As time went by and I was sailing more and more, it helped the business and I then thought it was time for the Company to pay my wages at all times; the owners then just paid my expenses. It is nice to think that it works both ways, because experience gathered all over the world stands the Company to good effect in the office. And of course I bring quite useful customers from time to time.

My very first professional job was as a deckhand in 1946 aboard the 96-foot ketch *Leander*, owned by a retired air commodore by the name of Howard-Williams. There were four of us lads, all about the age of fourteen (school leaving age in those days) and we lived on board. We were paid five shillings a week, half of which went into the bank, and the other half was used visiting my mother on my half day off every Wednesday. We didn't do a lot of sailing, though we went to the Channel Islands once or twice, but I learned something about a regular yacht's routine in the pre-war manner, because the owner and his wife were keen on discipline. The Channel Islands lie a day's sail across the relatively open waters of the English Channel, as most of my readers will know. They are quite close to the coast of France, and these trips represented my first experience of being outside England proper and thus were a great thrill for a young teenager. I remember particularly being impressed by the great rise and fall of tide at Guernsey, where the water level changes by nearly thirty feet at springs, so you have to tend your mooring lines regularly when tied alongside the quay.

From *Leander* I moved to *Clover*, which was a beautiful double ender owned by a man called Thompson, who made his money from beer bottle tops. My wages rose to £1 a week, which was a lot of money in 1947, and once again I lived on board with all found. One of my extra duties was that of cook, and I can't say that the food was very good. On one occasion I recall filling the paraffin tank over the cooker with liberal generosity, so that the evil smelling oil splashed all round the galley.

'I hope we don't have this flavour food every day,' remarked Mr Thompson as I cleared the lunch from the saloon table. When it came to my turn to eat, I realised with horror what he meant, for the taste of paraffin was in everything. So you can take it that cooking was not (nor is) one of my better accomplishments.

The next move was to *Mingary* for a couple of years, to continue the process of growing up and learning the life of a professional. We got up at dawn and scrubbed decks, leathered all the brightwork and polished the brass before breakfast. Then, if it rained, we went back up and leathered it all down again. I honestly don't think I'd have got where I am today if my introduction had not been started off the hard way; youngsters always have high spirits, and a bit of discipline never did anyone any harm. We put in a lot of sea time in *Mingary*, because the owner used to charter, so we were for ever popping across the Channel to Cherbourg and the Channel Islands.

## Racing

My first racing boat was the *Thistle*, a 6-metre owned by a Mrs Dreyfus, a keen yachtswoman who was good on the helm. The sixes were a hot class in those immediate post-war years, each boat had a couple of professionals on board, and you could really keep them up together. We laid at Fairey Marine at the mouth of the River Hamble, which meant that we had an hour's sail across to Cowes every Saturday and Sunday, and an hour's sail back. Then on Monday we used to haul her out, scrub down the enamel bottom and launch off again on the Friday.

Those 6-metre days gave me some of the best racing I ever had in my life. Apart from the boat-for-boat aspect of it, any one man on board could do any one job: he could gybe the spinnaker, sheet in the genoa, or hand any sail. The International One-Designs, which gave me my next job, were the same, except that they did not have such big spinnakers or jibs–the idea behind them was to provide a one-design 6-metre which could be raced by a family or taken away for a weekend's cruising. As often happens with successful dual purpose boats, they didn't do much cruising (the Dragon is another example of the same idea).

IOD's were all built in Norway to the design of Bjorn Aas, and there were fleets in Norway, Bermuda and UK. Now you might think that this is international enough, but the funny thing about IOD's was that they were neither international nor one-design, because each of the three fleets was different in minor respects from the other two (principally in size of sails). But they gave good, if unadventurous, racing–for one thing, the British boats never raced anywhere but out of Cowes. In the interests of economy, the class was only allowed one paid hand in each boat. This meant that those boats like ours, which was kept on the River Hamble, had to be sailed over to Cowes single handed, ready to meet the owner on Saturdays. Of course, they had no engine, so it meant that you had to do everything under sail, no bad thing for a youngster learning his trade, I would say. It meant getting the hang of how to handle a boat by feel at an early age, how to sail up to moorings under all conditions of wind and tide, and how to be self reliant.

Mark you, it didn't always work out. If you were coming up to your buoy down wind, you had to get the mainsail off just right, because if you judged it wrong the jib was so small that it often wasn't enough to pull her over the tide. You then had to haul up the mainsail again and have another go–and answer to the ribbing of your fellow professionals in the pub that evening, because you can bet they were all watching critically. I remember once picking up my buoy with a bit too much way on. It was low water, so the

moorings had a bit more scope than usual. Anyway, I got the eye of the line over the cleat, but we carried on and hit the Dragon on the next mooring.

'I see you had a bit of trouble,' said the owner when he came aboard. 'What do we do now?'

'Tell the owner of the Dragon to get her repaired at the yard, sir,' I answered. 'Then you pay his bill.'

And it was as easy as that! My owner was the first to recognise that this was the sort of thing which could happen to anyone sailing single handed week in and week out, and that it was part of the price of his sailing.

That was John Millar. I worked for him from 1954 to 1960, in a variety of boats. Besides a converted 8-metre called *Maid of Honour*, he had a 35-foot waterline boat called *Merry Dancer*, designed and built by Fife of Scotland, and later an IOD, which was called *Sybil*, after his daughter. He ran a factory which made aircraft parts in Hemel Hempstead, and later started a small business in the south of England to make yacht fittings, which proved to be my introduction to the business which has been my living ever since.

## American Waters

Mr Millar had an American wife and he also ran a business in the USA making aircraft components. In 1955 he was living in Newport, Rhode Island, and he decided to charter a boat called *Palawan* for the following season, in order to do some racing round the cans. So he sold both his boats at the end of the summer and told me to get ready to spend the next season in America.

'What about this winter, sir?' I asked. 'There'll be no boats to work on. What do I do then?'

'Dig your garden, paint your house and draw full pay from me,' he replied. 'There will then be no excuse for not being ready to go in the spring.'

So I spent the best part of eight months digging, planting, painting and decorating. In the end I was bored with it and eager to go. My wife gave birth to our daughter at this time, and it was all safely over and out of the way before I left for America, so that was convenient. It also gave her something to interest her while I was away (and neatly got me out of all the chores associated with new-born babies).

1956, therefore, saw me flying the Atlantic to race for the first time in American waters. *Palawan* was a beautiful 47-foot racing yawl designed by Sparkman and Stephens, and normally kept at Long Island by her owner Thomas J Watson Jnr. She had a good racing record having, among other successes, been first in Class B in the Annapolis–New London race the previous year. We had her up at Newport, and she easily outclassed everything up there. We won pretty well everything, and also cruised to Cape Cod and Martha's Vineyard. John Millar was delighted, because he was

very proud to be British and, though he liked the Americans very much, he liked better to beat them.

The general standard of equipment in the racing fleets out there was impressive. All the American gear was well ahead of the British equivalent, and Mr Millar was quick to spot this. That is what gave him the idea to start Avica, his marine fittings business in England. For instance, we were the first people to make spinnaker pole cups in UK, an idea which we had noticed on the American boats in 1956. We also imported their bronze turn-buckles, but Mr Millar went one better than the Americans, for he later had these made in Superston, a material which is stronger than stainless steel. We then tried our hands at pre-fabricated pulpits with press fitted joints (which failed to catch on). Almost all the American boats we saw had a good range of instruments as standard items. But one thing we did show them in Newport was the spinnaker turtle. I had used this on the IOD in England in 1955 and had one made for *Palawan* the following year. I understand that Philip Benson of Marblehead is generally credited with being the inventor of this wonderful device. He probably was, but they did not know about it in Newport in 1956, and ours caused quite a stir.

'I'll get my chap Parker to show you,' John Millar used to say in his ultra-British manner, when the Americans asked him about this secret weapon. One weekend when *Palawan* was not racing, I was invited aboard one of the other yachts and was offered ten dollars to bring the turtle with me. So I earned a few easy drinks out of it.

Racing was not quite so business-like in those days, even in America. We used to get a crew of young college lads keen for a bit of fun but, as soon as we started winning, they got more serious. We never had any trouble raising the numbers, in fact they lined up to join us. I may say that this was not only because of the success we had. These lads had never tasted hot tea made in the English way before, and they watched fascinated as I carefully heated the pot before pouring the boiling water onto the leaves (always taking the pot to the kettle, so that the water should be still boiling as it went into the pot). Then, after allowing the tea to brew for just the right length of time, I served it up. They loved it, and used to make it a condition of coming with us that I should make tea 'the Limey way'.

Ashore, I was always rigged out in the traditional British professional gear: dark blue suit, brass buttons and peaked hat. The Americans, who were accustomed to their paid hands being dressed in khaki drill, fell for this gear of mine, and just loved having me in their yacht clubs. They were, and are, wonderful people, and their legendary hospitality lives up to its own reputation. That was a marvellous season.

Back in England, Mr Millar bought *Knoel III*, a secondhand IOD, to be going on with, but he kept his promise to me and the following year we took delivery of a brand new, shining varnished

Fig 3. The beautiful yawl *Palawan*, from the board of Sparkman and Stephens, which gave me my first taste of racing in American waters in 1956.

IOD, which he called *Sybil* after his daughter. He also bought an old converted steam pinnace, which he took out to the USA for the America's Cup racing when *Sceptre* got so badly beaten in 1958. The Americans all wanted to buy her, but that was just the thing to make John Millar bring her all the way back to England again.

## Yacht Fittings

All this time we were improving the fittings in our boats, because we had the chance to see what the Americans were doing. I got keen on fittings, because deep down it gradually became obvious that a revolution was taking place. Modern materials meant that gear could be both lighter and more efficient. So in 1960 I went to work full time for Lewmar Marine in Emsworth on the south coast. As it happens, things did not work out too well, so I started looking around. One weekend I happened to come across an old friend of mine, Chippy Davy, who was varnishing his 26-foot Folkboat sloop. Now, if there's one thing I pride myself on, that's varnishing; I reckon I can get a pretty good finish with a varnish brush. So I stood and watched him for a bit, and he wasn't so bad himself, so we got talking. He was with Montague Smith at the time, and they were agents for Lewmar and, as it happens, Avica. Things were a bit slow, he said.

'Do you want anyone else to help you do nothing,' I asked.

'You serious?' he replied. So I told him I was thinking of leaving Lewmar and wouldn't mind trying my hand at selling paint and fittings. Chippy's answer was non-committal and I heard nothing more. Three weeks later my wife reminded him of our conversation, which he had apparently not taken as a real enquiry. Anyway, he approached his bosses, the Ryland brothers who worked in the heart of the manufacturing midland area of England, and that same week I went up for interview. They gave me a job the same day and I have been happily with them ever since.

Before closing this chapter, I might perhaps tell you the story of how a young man who had a rather high opinion of himself was brought down to earth. When polyurethane varnish first came on the market, it had to be sold in two different pots which needed to be mixed and then applied straight away as it started to go off quickly. Rylard Paints (That's not a misprint. The family name is Ryland, but the commercial name for their paint and varnish is Rylard, being a contraction of the brothers Ryland's hard enamel) developed a one-pot polyurethane which would do away with the bother of mixing, and with the inability to store it once the two pots had been put together. We wanted to get this new varnish onto a good boat, and selected a One-Tonner which was building at Port Hamble near our Southampton office. It was important to have the new product put on right so our hero, who fancied himself at the job, offered to do it and I positively encouraged him–you see, we were certain that he was the right man to get the best finish from this special development of ours, because the regular painters in the yard would not apply it as carefully and expertly as he could. After a certain amount of haggling and fuss over union rules, the men agreed to let our man do it, largely because we were making no charge.

Well, this chap got down to it with a will, and laid on the revolutionary polyurethane with an enthusiastic brush. The trouble was, he was too enthusiastic and put on too thick a coat. Those of you who have ever wielded a paint brush in anger will know that, while the result looks wonderful immediately after the coat is applied, this causes the varnish to collect in runs down the vertical sides of the boat; when it starts to dry there are so-called 'curtains' visible all over the surface. Needless to say, the men in the yard were full of glee and, when this 'expert' went back next day to start the long job of rubbing down to remove all traces of his poor handiwork, a sign leaning against the boat greeted me–yes, it was me.

## CURTAINS BY RYLARD

It took me a week to make it all good, and it will take the rest of my life to live it down–they have never let me forget. Which is a good thing, because you should learn from episodes like this, and I can certainly say that I tried to learn something for my later life from all the different jobs I did in those days, good or bad.

# two  Competition

After coming back from America I gave up full time professional yachting, as I told you in the previous chapter. Obviously there was no way I could work for Lewmar or, later, for Montague Smith and also be a permanent paid skipper seven days a week.

When Mr Millar had told me to take half the season and all the winter off prior to our American trip, I met Mr Guy Bowles at Fairey Marine one day, and he asked whether I could look after his boat *Gay Gauntlet* in my spare time–of which there was plenty, as you will have realised. Guy Bowles and John Millar were good friends, and Mr Bowles used to come sailing with us from time to time in *Sybil* and *Maid of Honour*, so it was soon fixed up between us. That was my first introduction to the man who I always maintain was the finest helmsman I ever sailed with–but more of that later.

I went on racing as John Millar's full time professional until I joined Lewmar in 1960, putting in the odd race with Guy Bowles whenever Mr Millar did not want me. As soon as I took a full time job in the sailing industry, I had to give up being a permanent skipper, though I still turned out in *Sybil* at weekends. But the owner obviously wanted someone full time, so we parted company and I moved on a part time basis to Mr Bowles and *Gay Gauntlet*.

## The Sunmaids

Mr Bowles had a new boat built during the winter of 1960/61. She was a sister ship to the Nicholson designed *Jolina* which had been pretty successful in 1960, and we called her *Sunmaid III*. We built in wood at Clare Lallows in Cowes, alongside another *Jolina*; the difference was that we were ⅞ths rig while the other one was masthead.

Now, there was considerable speculation as to which would prove the better boat on handicap. In those days, most designs were still ¾ or ⅞ths rig, and not a lot was known in England about the new masthead concept. So we all waited for the proof which would come when the two vessels were matched one against the other.

We didn't have long to wait. *Sunmaid III* was virtually outclassed and never really got a look in. It was all rather depressing, for we knew that our only chance of beating the other

Fig 4. *Sunmaid IV* reaching with full genoa under the spinnaker in 1963; I have the spinnaker sheet in the pulpit, so that I can see the luffs of both sails. You will have to take my word for it that the boat astern only has a spinnaker staysail as secondary sail.
*Photo: Eileen Ramsay*

*Jolina* was in a blow. Well, we soldiered on all that season, having to be content with second guns most of the time and only getting the occasional first. We sold her at the end of the year (when I say 'we sold her', don't get the impression that anyone but Mr Bowles owned *Sunmaid III*, but you get pretty possessive about any boat you sail in regularly so, when she is sold, it's 'we' who sell her. 'We' don't get the money, though, but you have to remember that 'we' haven't been paying any of the bills either).

Anyway, Guy Bowles decided we had to go to masthead rig, and the fibreglass Nicholson 36′ took his fancy. So he bought a hull from Halmatic of Havant, and got Clare Lallow to finish it off for him. *Sunmaid IV* was launched for the 1962 season, and was immediately successful. Looking back through my records, I find that we had 113 flags out of 123 starts in three seasons.

As I said, Guy Bowles was a fine helmsman. Right from the beginning of our relationship we got on well together, better than anyone else I have ever sailed with. He loved helming, particularly to windward, and was probably glad to be rid of the tactical running of the boat. For my part, I was delighted to find somebody who was clearly happy to settle to the helm and concentrate on getting the best out of the boat, without having to worry about where she was going. His concentration was such that he could shut out all outside events, and it was my job to see that nothing happened to disturb that concentration. We would beat to windward together, Guy Bowles feeling her along and me telling him anything he needed to know. If another boat was doing well under our lee, I would suggest that Mr Bowles should sail her full and by, to push her along a bit; if one was coming up on our weather, he was told to squeeze her up a bit.

There is no doubt that most people need to put everything they've got into concentrating on going to windward. Guy Bowles trusted me so implicitly that he could do this, while I talked him through the tactics, telling him when to tack, when to pinch and when to sail free. On one occasion he squeezed along a shore in Bournemouth Bay, just keeping off the beach to cheat the tide.

'Well done, Guy,' called one of his friends, when we came ashore after winning. 'I thought you were never going to clear that pier— nearest thing I've seen in years.'

'What pier?' was the answer. And he really had not seen it.

## Social

I suppose that I can date my personal involvement in the social side of racing from those days. You have to remember that I was at heart still very much a paid hand at that time, if not in fact, with a mental attitude which told me where the boundaries lay. But I remember with some affection racing to Le Havre in France. We won, and Guy Bowles would have nothing less than that I should join his party at the yacht club for the prize giving dinner. I was all tricked out in my blue suit and very much on my best behaviour, as

Fig 5. Prize-giving
dinner at the Deauville
casino in the early
1960's. Chippy Davy is on
the extreme left and the
young man with his back
to the radiator and the
frightened expression is
myself.

you may imagine, mixing with the 'gentry' as I was. All the more surprising, therefore, to see Mr Bowles take off his jacket after dinner because it was rather hot–gentlemen didn't do that in those days, and he also surprised a few of the other owners. But in five minutes they were all laughing and copying him, so what could I do? I shed my coat and a few prejudices at the same time. I had started to grow up.

From then on, wherever Guy Bowles went when sailing, I went too–cocktail parties, swimming pools, prize givings, the lot. It was my first experience of being part of a team, and I loved it. As I had only the one brass buttoned shore-going suit, it soon became apparent to me that I needed a reefer, grey flannels and a rather more nautical tie than those which I had at home, so I joined the local sailing club.

## Keenness

One of my firm rules aboard any boat where I am sailing master has always been to make the crew aware of the need for the helmsman to concentrate. If you are content with a middle-of-the-fleet position, just beating your particular buddy, then by all means take it easy, enliven the day with lighthearted banter, and take beer and sandwiches as a welcome relaxation at the helm. But if you want to win, then there must be no chatter from the crew where the helmsman can hear; absolute silence must prevail around the cockpit except for the voice of the tactician.

Mark you, we were one of the few boats in those days to practise this somewhat spartan régime. But it paid off, as the results show. It was called keenness then, but it has gone a stage further these days, and it is a cut-throat game now. To give you an idea, we had only one genoa and one spinnaker aboard *Sunmaid* for quite a while and, if the spinnaker tore, we took it down, mended it and put it up again. We did eventually order a light genoa, but Mr Bowles was not sufficiently confident to go to a top class loft. The result was a terrible shape, and he pulled the sailmaker's leg about making us a cover for a hay rick. But it certainly made her go, and he cheerfully paid the bill when it came in made out 'Sum due, for one rick cover...'

It is almost unbelievable to remember now how we set the mainsail: it was hauled up, the clew was pulled out and made fast, and there it stayed for the rest of the race without further adjustment–unless we had to reef. The same went for our one and only genoa, though in this case I did realise the importance of a tight luff for windward work, and I used to jump on the winch handle to get that last notch or two on the halyard when hoisting sail. But when it was up, there it stayed. We had no slack luff jibs, no spinnaker staysail, no tallboy or anything else–until *Hestia* came over from Holland and frightened the life out of us. But I am getting ahead of my story.

This was a fascinating period of change. The old order of

hoisting sail and working sedately round the course, using skill at
the helm to take advantage of wind shifts, and tactical acumen to
exploit the tides, was about to go for ever. We ourselves were
groping on the edge of becoming cut-throat competitors in our
approach to racing, but we were still only beginners. We had
single-speed winches, for the genoa only, with big diameter drums
adapted from the 6-metres; there were no spinnaker sheet winches,
and we pulled this sail up by hand all the way. But I had been
impressed by Mr Bowles' obsession with beating to windward; he
used to reckon the race won or lost on the upwind legs and always
handed over the helm at the weather mark. This was no bad thing
in its way, for it enabled him to get refreshed for the next stint of
hard concentration when we came on the wind again. But I got to
thinking that, if we could gain ground upwind, we ought to be able
to do the same to leeward.

The result of all this brainwork was that we were the first to
increase our area downwind by carrying the genoa with the
spinnaker. British boats tended at this time to be undercanvassed,
and our experiment paid off immediately, for we started picking off
our rivals one after the other. You had to adopt a new approach to
sail trim, mark you, because it proved to be as important to watch
the luff of the spinnaker downwind as it was to concentrate on the
luff of the genoa to windward. If the spinnaker got too close to the
genoa they interfered with one another; if they were too far apart,
it usually meant that the spinnaker sheet was too slack and the sail
collapsed. It quickly became apparent that the sheet trimmer had
to be stationed where he could see both the luff of the spinnaker
and the genoa all the time. During an early cross Channel race to
Cherbourg, I remember going into the pulpit as dusk fell, to trim
the spinnaker and call the genoa. They brought me tea and
sandwiches, and it was dawn before the course changed enough to
cause the spinnaker to come down, so that I could leave my self-
appointed post.

A significant factor quickly became evident: a quivering luff to
the spinnaker was not always a sign that the sheet needed to be
hardened–sometimes it was necessary to ease it so that the airflow
between the spinnaker and genoa had a clean run; not everyone
appreciated this. Of course, we quickly had our imitators, but none
of our rivals seemed to get the hang of things as early as we had;
perhaps they failed to concentrate as much, or perhaps we were
just lucky. It got to the point where we would see a competitor
alongside us hoist his genoa under his spinnaker.

'It's all right, sir,' I would say to the owner. 'We've got him now,
he'll start falling astern of us.'

And he usually did.


**New Gear**

This success caused Mr Bowles to decide on fitting special
spinnaker sheet winches. Up to then, we had cleated the genoa and

used the same winch for the spinnaker sheet, but this caused a certain amount of bother and, in any case, the lead was none too good for working from the weather deck. So we had a word with that great engineer Len Lewery who, with Leslie Marsh, had started Lew-mar Marine. He quickly developed small winches suitable for the job, and we fitted them at the after end of the cockpit. We had started to improve, and from now on we were really in business. We carried the genoa under the spinnaker whenever possible, even if it meant sailing three or four degrees further off the wind; on a hundred mile leg you can afford to do this for an hour or so if it gives you another knot, because you can always make it up later. Only three or four degrees, mind, not ten or fifteen.

Now, the best incentive to make a boat go better is to get beaten. Well, the following year Peter Nicholson, that very capable follower of his father and grandfather, came out with another Nick 36–and thus a sister ship to us–which he called *Janessa*. This gave us the competition we needed if we were not to become complacent. The first surprise he gave us was to reduce the length of his spreaders by six inches or so, to enable him to sheet his genoa that little bit closer. So we cut ours down even more to beat him (without any reference, I may say, to the mast maker or the rigger, who would probably have thrown up their hands in horror at this flouting of the 11 degrees minimum angle rule). Then Peter put battens in his genoa to get more roach area (there was no rule about it in those days). We then decided to have one of the first deck sweeping genoas; this meant that we had to reduce the height of the lifelines forward, or the sail would not have sheeted; so we cut our first two stanchions down to six inches (again there was no rule), thus forcing *Janessa* to do the same. When the RORC brought in the very sensible rule requiring unbroken lifelines two feet high all round the boat (our six inch lines were nothing more than trip wires–in fact, I did just that one Cowes Week, and went straight over the side), we angled our stanchions 15–20 degrees outboard to allow the genoa to be trimmed inside the lifeline; this meant that we had to take out the split pins when we came alongside, so we could turn the stanchions inboard so as not to foul the jetty, but we were striving for performance all the time. Peter Nicholson replied by moving his chainplates inboard, again so he could trim his genoa between the shrouds and the lifelines. We copied the Americans and shaved the rather bluff forward end to our keel into a knife edge, putting the lead we removed back into the boat inside the hull, just above where we had taken it off. I don't know whether it did us any good, but we felt we were improving all along, and that's a large part of the battle.

I have gone into some detail about this changing of layouts, merely to show that we were spurred on by each other, alert to the possibilities of exploiting the rules, and determined to do everything within those rules to gain speed. Now, you may say that we should have sailed to the spirit of the rule rather than the letter,

Fig 6. An unusual shot, distorted by the fish-eye lens, of *Sunmaid V*, showing her three halyard winches mounted on the coachroof. Left to right are self, Bill Bowles (the owner's son), Royston Comport then of Ratsey and Lapthorn, and Guy Bowles. *Photo: Lewmar*

and I'm not going to say that you are wrong. But at the time, the spirit of competition and the keenness to improve were such that I don't think we would have given this idea five seconds reflection. As it happens, it never crossed our minds to consider the wider issues. We in *Sunmaid* were out to beat *Janessa*, and I think that Peter Nicholson and his crew thought little of anything other than putting one over on us next Saturday. And this is the way it should be, for out of it all comes eventual improvement for everybody. Mark you, it is also quite right and proper that some authority ('they', I suppose you could say) should take note of what we were doing, and put the brakes on when things looked like getting out of hand. But you cannot ask us to respect the spirit of the rule and, in the same breath, demand to know why we lack the dedicated approach thus letting other countries get ahead when it comes to finding useful gaps in the complicated measurement regulations.

To sum it up, this was the year that *Sunmaid IV* did not have it all her own way, and I remember it as a year of intense interest and also one of intense pleasure whenever we managed to beat Peter Nicholson. It was a joy to pit ourselves against a great competitor and we had some super racing. If Peter had not given us the incentive, I'm sure that we would have gone on in the same old rut, and half the ideas we produced between us would never have seen the light of day anywhere near so soon.

I may say that we didn't rest on our laurels because, when Guy Bowles later bought *Sunmaid V*, a Sparkman & Stephens One-Tonner, we got down to trapezing until we were (thankfully) stopped by a change in the rules. Funnily enough, the first *Morning Cloud* was a direct descendant of this boat because Olin Stephens drew inspiration from *Sunmaid* for Mike Winfield's *Morningtown*, which in turn led to the slightly smaller S&S 34 production class, of which *Morning Cloud* was the most famous example.

## Twin Boom Gybe

Since we are talking of development, we might as well look back at the introduction of the twin boom spinnaker gybe. This was started by Chippy Davy and myself sitting in the Montague Smith office one day, and pondering the problems of the foredeck hand as he tried to control the spinnaker boom in the struggle to switch it from one clew to the other in a gusting wind. We got the idea that it should be possible to rig a second boom with a short strop from the old clew, taken along the boom itself to a cleat near the inner end; this would take the place of the guy, and would avoid the need to wrestle with an unconnected boom hooked onto the sail, which could take charge at any moment. We put the idea to John Oakeley, who worked with Proctor Metal Masts at that time, and asked him to work on the details. To cut a long story short, he came up with the idea that our strop would, in fact, be better if it were turned into a fully working duplicate guy which could be trimmed as a permanency on the new gybe. We developed the gear and turned the idea into practice between us.

And it worked!

Soon all the British boats which wanted to stay up front were copying us: short spreaders, lower stanchions, inboard shrouds, deck-sweeping genoas with battens, twin boom gybe–the lot. We thought we were forging ahead by leaps and bounds. In fact next year, 1964, when I was skipper of *Kurrewa*, one of the British contenders for the America's Cup challenge, we thought we were so far ahead of the Americans in gear and drill that there would be no contest. We were due for a shock, but that is another chapter. For the immediate problem, the Americans didn't go all that heavy on the twin boom gybe; they had evolved their own method, which became known as the dip pole system. It was quicker and took less gear (always a pointer to simplicity), but it needed a man in the pulpit who was sure handed, and it needed complete control of the after guy, topping lift, downhaul and new guy. But this is the eternal strength of the Americans: they breed good crewmen, who can work to a pattern without mistakes.

So we developed two different methods on each side of the Atlantic. When we went over to Rhode Island for the 1964 challenge, *Sovereign* used the dip pole system, while we in *Kurrewa* operated the twin boom arrangement. We raced fairly level, the results in British waters being 12–11 in our favour before we left for the USA, where *Sovereign* took the final trials 4–2. We shall come on to all that later, but it was interesting to compare gybe systems in close competition. It seemed to me that *Sovereign* had the edge in light winds, but that the greater control offered by the twin pole method paid off in heavy weather. We could set up our second spinnaker pole without any weight on it, draw the spinnaker clew down to the boom end, and then release the old pole (which could be stowed at leisure–if such a luxury can ever be said to exist on a racing twelve), without having the spinnaker with two loose clews at any time, or needing to fight the new guy into the pole end fitting against a snatching wind. With the introduction of bendy spars, baby stays and inner stays (which cannot always be released in a blow, without risk to the somewhat thin section masts), boats have had to go back to the twin boom gybe anyway, because the pole cannot dip through the fore triangle. So you pay your money and take your choice: one forestay and dip pole gybe; or bendy mast, baby stay and the twin pole set-up. I prefer the latter, but then I'm prejudiced and I would never stop an owner from going for the former, if that is what he wanted.

## Sails

I referred earlier to *Hestia's* part in this revolution–perhaps I should call it an evolution–of ideas and gear. As I have said already, British boats tended to be undercanvassed in those days,

largely as a result of our somewhat boisterous conditions outside
coastal waters. We were also quite content in those days to set our
sails at the start of a race and leave them severely alone until we
had crossed the finishing line. Then Mr van Beuningen came over
from Holland with his Sparkman and Stephens designed *Hestia*, no
beamier than the Nicholson 36', though slightly shorter and a good
bit lighter. He packed a lockerful of headsails, which he ran up and
down the forestay with alarming agility to suit every wind change.
He had light genoas, spinnaker staysails, intermediate genoas and
even at one time a three-clewed quadrilateral (still allowed by the
rule in those days).

This made us look up, I can tell you, for we weren't used to all
this switching and changing. So once again our hands were forced
and, if we wanted to stay up front, we had to join the chase. Thus
we added to the faithful genoa which had done us so well for two
seasons, and we got a light weather sail–the 'rick cover' I
mentioned earlier; we invested in one of the new-fangled rope luff
genoas where we could control the flow in the sail; we bought ('we'
again; I certainly didn't help pay for it) a spinnaker staysail–
which did not last long, for we went better under full genoa when
we had the spinnaker up; and we even tried a quadrilateral, but I
was glad when the rule outlawed them.

Perhaps the principal change forced on us was the double head
rig off the wind. This was before the days of the really close
reaching spinnaker (star-cut, genniker, spanker, tri-radial–call it
what you like), and we needed extra canvas on a close fetch if we
were to stay with *Hestia*. So we set up an inner forestay and hoisted
a second headsail, and had fun sorting out the relationship of the
three sails and their sheet leads.

# three  The America's Cup

To any sailing man, the chance to be part of a challenge for the America's Cup must be a high spot. I'm not saying that 12-metres are the finest boats afloat, nor is there any point in becoming involved in discussion on the merits of this competition between dinosaurs; I don't even want to put forward my ideas on how this particular racing should be run. Like it or lump it, like Mount Everest it's there, and it is a privilege to have helped have a go at it and thus to have helped improvement in gear and design.

## Planning

After World War II, it was not until 1958 that Britain was ready to mount the seventeenth challenge for the trophy which has been described as one of the ugliest in existence (Victoriana is staging a come-back, however, and we may yet learn to admire its ornate magnificence); at all events, like an aloof woman, it is almost mockingly desirable, and rich men have spent fortunes in its pursuit and defence. *Sceptre's* abortive effort is well enough documented elsewhere to need no further comment from me, except to say that thereafter it was even more important that any further challenge should give a good account of itself. In the early sixties Lord Craigmyle formed the Red Duster syndicate but, apart from an almost entirely rebuilt pre-war 12-metre, all he had to show for the six figure sum at which he called a halt was some test tank and wind tunnel data. Then Mr Tony Boyden brought three years of careful planning to a climax by having a new boat designed by Alan Boyd (who, though he had been responsible for the unfortunate *Sceptre*, was a successful 6-metre designer and the only naval architect in the country with recent 12-metre experience), and she was christened *Sovereign* at her launching in 1963; a golden sovereign was placed under the heel of her mast for good luck.

It was clear that a second boat was desirable if not essential, if only to show the Americans that we were serious, and eventually the brothers Frank and John Livingstone said that they would put up the money to buy the boat if somebody else would campaign her; Mr Owen Aisher said that he was willing, and so it was arranged. Now, Stan Bishop had been Mr Aisher's skipper for years, and he was earmarked for the same job aboard *Kurrewa V*, as the boat was to be called. Sadly he died, and Mr Aisher kindly offered me the post (I had already agreed to be foredeck chief under Stan). This was a proud moment for me, and it is sad that my father was not able to see it, for he had been a crew member of *Endeavour* when she tried to get the cup from *Rainbow* back in 1934. This, of course, was the famous series when the cup came nearest to changing hands. *Endeavour* won the first two races and, in the third, she was a mile ahead of *Rainbow* and only the same distance short of the line when the wind died away. Harold S Vanderbildt and his skipper Starling Burgess hung their heads in shame and went below, confessing that they had lost the cup, while Sherman Hoyt took the wheel with the old cry that no race is lost until it is over. After some time, Sir Thomas Sopwith on board *Endeavour* could resist temptation no longer and went off in search of wind, instead of staying between *Rainbow* and the finish. The wind came up all right, but in the area Sopwith had just left, so that the Americans sailed home and won. They did some rapid gear changing with some of the other potential defenders, altered their ballast and went on to retain the trophy.

To get back to our challenge, the Livingstone brothers were Australian sheep farmers who had done a good deal of sailing earlier in life, including crossing the Pacific. Then in their early sixties, they were content at that time to spend their money 'so that they could watch others enjoying themselves', as they put it; this was money well spent according to them. Their first *Kurrewa* (the name means a fast Australian fish) was a 16-footer which they had built themselves 50 years previously; in between they raced various *Kurrewas* in the Sydney–Hobart, the trans-Tasman (1200 miles) and the Los Angeles-Honolulu races (usually sailing their boat to get to the starting port). Their reason for putting their money behind a British boat, rather than an Australian one, was their fear that the rules of the competition on which they had set their hearts would prevent another challenge for some years, following the *Gretel* campaign in 1962, and 'we're not getting any younger, you know.'

*Kurrewa V* was a near sister to *Sovereign*, as Mr Boyden had kindly allowed the plans to be reproduced by Alan Boyd, and she was not launched until 1964 (Don't ask me to comment on whether a completely new design would have been a better idea. There just wasn't time, so that fortunately puts an end to that speculation). This meant that we only had that summer to tune up, get the crew working as a team, and give *Sovereign* (who had been sailing since the previous year) a run for her money before we had to go out to America for the races in September. A golden guinea was placed under the heel of our mast, in the hope that its five per cent extra value on *Sovereign's* coin would be translated into a similar margin of speed.

## Elimination Trials

Peter Scott and Erik Maxwell shared the wheel on *Sovereign*, while our helmsman was Col Stug Perry, who had won a silver medal in the 5.5-metres at the 1956 Olympics. To jump ahead of myself with the knowledge of hindsight (a somewhat clumsy exercise, you will agree), Peter Scott was a brilliant helmsman somewhat out of practice, and Col Perry was nearer 60 than 50, so perhaps was no longer quite up to the verve he had shown eight years earlier at Melbourne.

But all that was to come. The two boats settled down to trials off the Nab Tower east of the Isle of Wight, where it was thought that conditions most nearly approached the notorious swell in which the actual cup races would be conducted; there were some, including Mr Boyden, who would have preferred the open waters off Weymouth–and events proved them to be not so far wrong. The boats, of course, were the height of technical perfection for those days, and virtually nothing we wanted was denied us–in the way of equipment I mean. Match racing is a fascinating, if slightly selfish, form of yacht racing. It is a different matter for the competitors, however, and I found it completely absorbing, but eventually felt that our respective helmsmen were beginning to know too much about each other. We would normally be correct in our guesswork as to *Sovereign's* tactics in any given situation, and there is no doubt that the same held good aboard our rivals. When the time came to race against the Americans, the challenger would obviously meet a whole new set of ideas, a situation neither helmsman nor the tactician had encountered for a long time.

Meanwhile we slugged it out with a will, one against the other, occasionally racing against *Sceptre* or even the re-built pre-war *Norsaga*, and of course there was the odd upset as one of the older boats stole a race. This was always made much of by the yachting correspondents at the time, but was usually the result of a freak set of circumstances. Freak that is, until right at the end of the tuning up series, when Jack Knights was able to write in the Sunday Express in June:

'Old *Sceptre* is sending chills down the spines of the crews of both these handsome and costly machines. Starting a few minutes behind, on Saturday *Sceptre* gained eleven minutes and on Sunday she gained nine. The apologists for the new yachts say that *Sceptre* is now faster than she was, that she is better sailed and better trimmed than in 1958. I just cannot believe that she could ever improve to the point where she could seriously hope to beat *Columbia*, let alone *American Eagle* who is so far unbeaten by any of the other four potential defenders.'

## Newport, Rhode Island

At the end of the British trials, both yachts were shipped to America in June for final eliminators under local conditions. At

Fig 7. *Kurrewa V* being crossed by *Sovereign*, who is getting ready to cover, in one of the early trial races. Note the tactician with his plotting board in the special cockpit behind the helmsman.
*Photo: Beken*

the time we were leading *Sovereign* by 12 races to 11, but I have to confess that some of our successes were achieved with a suit of Hood sails which Mr Aisher had bought for *Kurrewa*. We would not be allowed to use these for the challenge itself, but it was obvious that sails would play a big part in the battle, and Mr Aisher made them available for the British sailmakers to examine and learn from. At this time Hood's own sailcloth was so far superior to anything that we were weaving on this side of the Atlantic that we refused to believe it. According to the 'comfortable' theory, anything they could weave we could weave just as well. Admittedly, the American canvas was tight, firm and did not need resin fillers to cut down porosity and stabilise the cloth; but these were known requirements, and the British weavers had already declared that they could match Hood's cloth construction. In fact, we even had a shot or two in our locker, for one of the producers had developed a system of bonding two lightweight cloths together–plycloth they called it–in the hope that the result would not stretch so much under load. It didn't stretch much, but the bonding came apart in use, so it failed to live up to its hopes.

To be frank, we were behind in both sailcloth and sailmaking. Ted Hood used techniques which were so radical at that time that British boats, unused to setting such sails, were unable to hoist them properly. On several occasions Ted had been summoned by British owners and, indeed, designers, to cross the Atlantic in order to observe his so-called ill-fitting products. His regular answer was that he would come and, if the sails needed alteration, he would pay his own expenses; if he could set them to the owner's satisfaction, he would not expect to be out of pocket. In fact, he did more than that, for he used to tell the owners to hoist the sails one to two feet harder than they had been used to, before committing themselves to a return ticket across the Atlantic (I don't believe that Ted ever had to pay his own fare on any of these trips).

## Analysis of Failure

So off to Newport we went, full of high hopes. We really believed that our advances in equipment–some of which I have described earlier–were such that we would have more than an edge on the opposition. But of course, the Americans had not been standing still all this time and anything we might have surprised them with, such as the twin pole spinnaker gybe, was noted carefully by that great sailor Carleton Mitchell, who came across to Britain to see what we were doing during our warm-up racing (I suppose we should have expected this, for hadn't they sent a similar observer in 1937 and spotted *Endeavour II*'s quadrilateral jib being tried out south of the Isle of Wight?). In the event, the American twelves had little to fear for they were equipped about the same as ours, but they had several other enormous advantages working for them:

    1.  First, Hood's sails were far better than anything we could show. *Sovereign* had mostly Banks sails with the odd spinnaker

from Seahorse and some genoas and a mainsail from Ratsey & Lapthorn, while we in *Kurrewa* had nearly all Ratsey sails, with some Banks spinnakers and one of his mainsails. 12-metre spinnakers are unrestricted in measurement, and the vogue in England at the time was to cram as much area into them as possible, the theory being that you would get more thrust that way. But the Americans kept the size to reasonable proportions, with the result that their spinnakers generally set much better than ours, particularly in light winds, and were certainly easier to control. Both our boats found that their Banks radial reaching spinnakers gave excellent results, and these were not quite so large as the big down wind jumbos.

2.   Next, the American approach was more dedicated than ours, even allowing for a much more determined spirit in the British camp after *Sceptre*'s somewhat casual attitude. The 12-metre rule called for a cabin sole: we had pine boards stretching eight feet across the bottom of the boat; the Americans had eight *inches*. The rule demanded linings to the cabin sides: we had traditional British wooden linings; the Americans used nylon cloth. A toilet was required: we had the usual mahogany box, with beautiful dovetailed joinery; the Americans had a can nailed to the floor–or so it seemed. Rod and Olin Stephens invited us aboard the various American twelves quite soon after we arrived, and our eyes nearly popped out of our heads at their workmanlike appearance. At any event, we took 500 lb of wood out of *Kurrewa V* as soon as we had seen *Constellation*, *American Eagle* and the others, but of course this could only have been done efficiently at the construction stage.

3.   The Americans had five yachts competing for the honour of defending the cup. This gave them good competition, a strong pool of helmsmen and crews, a variety of tactics and a host of other advantages. For our part, we had two good boats, boundless enthusiasm and, as it turned out, a blissful ignorance of the fate awaiting us.

We had heard a lot about the particular swell which is a characteristic of the waters off Newport, Rhode Island, where the cup races were to be held. But this is something which is easy to dismiss when you have not experienced it; there is no doubt, however, that it plays an important part in the racing. At least three of *Sovereign*'s crew had sailed in *Sceptre* during the 1958 fiasco, but I don't know how much time Alan Boyd the designer had spent in twelves in those waters. We certainly did not do enough practice sailing in the actual race area, for we spent our first week in America at the Seawanhaka Yacht Club on Long Island, a hundred miles from Newport. Equally, nobody seems to have warned Peter Scott that the masthead vane, on which he placed a certain amount of reliance, would swing about so much in the swell as to render it virtually useless at times. Finally, I believe that neither of our boats gave her sails a proper chance to settle down. I'm not saying that they would have been good enough, but a new genoa would be tried and, particularly if the boat had lost, almost anybody felt free to criticise the cut of the cloth. The sail would then be immediately taken back to the loft and altered. By the time this had been done half a dozen times in as many days, the records of how the thing had been made must have been unintelligible. So nobody knew how to reproduce the final genoa, even if we had wanted to.

All this sounds like an apologia for failure. Well, I suppose any analysis of the factors behind a defeat is bound to add up to that. But make no mistake about it, we were keen, first to achieve the honour of actually challenging, then to back the boat which got selected, and finally to see that the challenge was well and truly made.

The final British selection trials in American waters started off well for *Sovereign*. She won the first three races and, in the end, they beat us over there by 4–2, making a total of 15–14 to them over the whole season in both UK and US waters. Stug Perry had begun by generally beating Peter Scott at the start, always an important part of match racing. But *Sovereign* learned from her mistakes, and soon they were giving us as good as they got, to the point where they eventually held their own with the Americans during the actual races. They deserved their selection, and we were glad to offer them any help we could–but now was not the time to make crew changes even had they wanted to, nor to start trying out those of our sails which fitted.

## Morale

There had been some criticism in the press of *Kurrewa*'s spinnaker drill. Among others, the *Daily Telegraph* reckoned that 'lack of spinnaker trimming skill had brought her to her knees.' I'm not necessarily agreeing that it was bad but, when the stakes are high and you are looking for improvement, you tend to react to any influence–did I hear somebody talk about clutching at straws? In any case, it would have been silly not to take any notice of the considered opinion of dispassionate experts. Now, Chippy Davy was one of the best spinnaker men in the business at that time, and I suggested that we should get him over to see whether he could help. Mr Aisher agreed immediately and Chippy flew out. His arrival was not exactly greeted with open arms by our afterguard, and I believe that Stug Perry was against it from the start, feeling that Chippy had less right aboard than crewmen from his own successful 5.5-metre who were also available. Certainly the Olympic bronze medal winners had all sailed together a good deal and their team work was not in question, but the call had gone to the man I had suggested, and it was up to us all to try to make it a success. Anyway, the first time Chippy came aboard was for a practice sail, between trials with *Sovereign*. Standing on the after deck, ready to observe our efforts, he was suddenly aware that he was being sharply spoken to.

'Put out that cigarette,' barked Perry. 'We don't allow smoking on board this boat.'

Now this was not strictly true, for one or two of the lads used to have a quick drag from time to time. But this was not the real point. Chippy had been made to feel like a schoolboy rebuked in front of his classmates. The atmosphere got more and more chilly as the day wore on until, when we tied up again, Chippy got off, packed his bags and flew home to England. He never had a chance to try anything and never even raced once with us.

It is sad to record that just a little lowering of spirit crept into our boat as the US trials progressed. Perhaps it was because we knew in our hearts that we were losing, but I also believe that failure to keep the whole crew together while ashore contributed. This was in marked contrast to Mr Heath's invariable practice in *Morning Cloud* later, as I have related elsewhere, and perhaps it is worth recording that I have never known a crew which stayed in the same hotel and attended all the same functions together to have a low morale. The bad patch did not last for long, and it was Mr Aisher's dominant spirit and superb treatment of us all which enabled us to shrug it off in the end.

'It will be Mr Aisher you'll be letting down if you quit,' I had to tell three of them. 'So unpack your bags and get stuck in.'

The rest is history. *Constellation* beat *Sovereign* in four straight races, despite Peter Scott taking the start on at least two occasions. Bob Bavier soon realised that he could afford to stay out of trouble, accept the less favourable initial berth if necessary, and still quickly sail into a commanding lead. It was noteworthy how the two rivals would start side by side, perhaps with *Sovereign* to windward, and sail level for about three or four minutes. Then Bavier would obviously get into the groove and slowly start edging ahead. This is the hallmark of a great helmsman, who settles to his task of concentrating on the job of sailing close hauled in complete silence; gradually he would get the feel of the wind and swell, settle into the slot and the boat became alive. Meanwhile Peter Scott, short of recent practice and possibly more at home in a dinghy than a thoroughbred keelboat, would be vainly groping for that magic touch to coax his charge along with inferior canvas. An additional factor was the somewhat erratic behaviour of the wind instruments, caused by the sea conditions. Bereft of his mechanical aids, Peter Scott was forced back to the feel of the wind on his cheeks–a method on which he was brought up, but which he had forsaken for the whole of two seasons just sailed, in favour of dials, and it was now too late to revert.

I left the scene after the first couple of races had showed me that there was little reason to stay behind. I supervised the packing up of our boat ready for the trip home, and then made my way back to England, sad to have failed but, as I said at the beginning of this chapter, both honoured and delighted to have been part of the challenge.

## The Future

I think that any future assault on this elusive trophy will need even greater dedication than we were able to offer. Winning will be a terrific job, needing not only thousands of man-hours, but also an enormous budget. The Admiral's Cup fleet is the obvious place to look for crews for any future British challenge, but I wonder how many men in the offshore fleet have what it takes to work a 12-metre to peak condition. A lot of the skills are similar, but there is an indefinable something which only seems to reach maturity in class racing such as in Solings or Dragons–perhaps it will emerge in the one-design offshore racers; it then has to be developed and exercised in the larger surroundings of a 12-metre itself, and this is where the Americans have a big advantage. They have a pool of some half a dozen top twelves, so they not only breed the right skills, but they have a good deal of the right racing to sharpen them up.

I would dearly love to see a successful British challenge, and only hope that one day it will come off. Certainly all efforts would have my best wishes, and I can only pray that the kind of disenchantment which we suffered is never again experienced by my countrymen. When I first saw the technological advances achieved by the Americans back in 1964, and I learned of the very high crewing standards of the defenders, my heart faltered for a moment or two–which is just what Rod and Olin had intended, I suppose. Next time, let's hope that it works the other way. Britain has spent enough effort chasing that Cup; the first time it has to be unscrewed from its temporary resting place in the New York Yacht Club, it would be poetic justice that it should return to the country where it all started.

# four **Business Life**

I don't want you to get the idea that my time is spent in one long round of sailing and racing–pleasant as this would be–so I'd better start telling you something of my business life. I have already briefly related my period as a professional yacht hand and how the decision was made to give up full time paid sailing. That sort of job is becoming more and more scarce these days, it demands very long hours, and is not always as well rewarded as it might be. Don't get the idea that I am afraid of work; those who know me realise that long hours have never worried me. But I wanted more variety and a greater challenge from life than was offered by being a yacht hand. Besides which, the rules of yacht racing make a difference between amateur and professional sailing, and it soon became apparent that some of the top competitions would be closed to me as a pro–in fact I still have a letter from the Royal Yachting Association telling me that I could not at that time be a crew member in the One-Ton Cup series.

So I gave up professional crewing and joined Lewmar in 1960, largely as a result of having seen something of that side of things with John Millar and his Avica business. From there the move to work with my old friend Chippy Davy came in 1961. The IYRU recognises that those engaged in the yachting industry need the experience of competitive sailing, and they allow amateur status to sailmakers, boat builders, chandlers and all the other businesses connected with sailing; broadly speaking, the line is drawn between those who make a living at crewing on a boat, and those who work in the industry to produce the boat and its equipment. My eventual application to regain amateur status was successful.

## Montague Smith

Montague Smith is a subsidiary of Llewellyn Ryland Ltd, and in 1961 they had the agencies for a number of products such as Henderson bilge pumps, the Avica range of equipment (of which we have already heard), Rylard paints of course, and Lewmar deck gear, besides a number of other small companies. Lewmar was, and remains, our biggest supplier, and we handled their full range of winches, blocks, cleats, stanchions and the like. Like us, they dealt direct with the customer as well as through agents, but they have since stopped trading other than through an intermediary; we hold their sole agency in the south of England.

There were six of us in the business at that time, and my job was basically that of a salesman, second in charge to Chippy. I was also general dogsbody, required to clean up the store, fetch the tea, deliver rush orders and generally to fill in if anyone else was away. But my main task was to build up the business.

We had an annual turnover of around £30,000 in those days and were only just in profit. But this was obviously not good enough, and clearly we were at the make or break point–we had to turn in better results or my future would be doubtful to put it mildly. So Chippy and I set to work even more doggedly than before, and got around that part of the country which was our patch with regularity and determination. Fortunately for us, this was the start of the development period of which I have already written. One-off wooden boats were already becoming hard to find in the building yards, and the first glimmerings of production line techniques could be seen. This was a big thing for us because, where yards used to build three or four boats a year, they were now turning out that many a month. So, instead of two dozen stanchions and bases a year, they were now buying 250. The same sort of increase held good for pulpits, winches, pumps and the rest of our range, so the man who could deliver the goods got the orders–always supposing that they were the right goods.

That's where our firm had the edge on some of the competition. We have always had super backing from the directors, provided we put up a good case. Anyway, the evidence that Chippy and I brought back from our sales trips showed clearly that quick delivery was becoming of prime importance. We asked for more investment in stock, backed it with figures, and got the money. The results were electrifying, and our turnover jumped with attendant profitability; we had turned the corner and our future was assured.

It looks easy, written down like that, but I can assure you that it wasn't. There were many times when Chippy and I would sit into the night, talking over the week's problems and possibilities, and wondering where we were going. Was this upsurge all a bubble? Would such and such a yard really build that number of boats? Were the boats what the public wanted? Would they sell them? In other words, would we get our money? Then, when that had been aired, where should we go on our next trips? Looking back on those times, I realise now what confidence Chippy placed in me and how he showed me the way and then gave me my head. He was a grand man to work with–I nearly said 'for', but that would do him an injustice, because there was never any question of boss and underling between us (although I always knew who was in charge, and who would take the biggest rap if we failed).

Another big point in our favour in those days of expansion was the fact that we dealt in high quality goods. Names like Rylard, Lewmar and Henderson are household words in the yachting business, and we were confident of our wares. What is more,

Chippy always believed in good after-sales service, and he made sure that I believed in it too. This is something which has paid off a thousand fold, and is now just another reason why I shall always remember that man with considerable affection.

In 1966 Chippy died of cancer and I was made manager. There was still a lot to be done, but the way was fairly clear to me and, as always, I had the most marvellous backing from Head Office. I decided that we should cut out our retail outlet, because it was not only absorbing a disproportionate amount of our time and effort, but tended to irritate the trade customers on whom we relied. For somewhat similar reasons it was also evident that some of the slow moving or restricted lines were proving unprofitable in the long term, so we dropped them. What we were doing, perhaps without realising it at the time, was streamlining the operation so that we could give quicker, better (and better backed) service to the customers who mattered: production boat builders, designers and chandlers.

At about this time Lewmar decided to go over to wholesaling only. Up till then they had also dealt with the builders and chandlers, so this had meant that our outlets were being tapped. On the other hand, it had also meant that Lewmar had to carry a disproportionately heavy overhead to operate the service, with the result that their prices were higher than they needed to be. Their principal competitor in the UK was M S Gibb Ltd, who have always put out a high quality product, so Lewmar had the healthy spur of competition to keep them efficient. They only gave up dealing direct, when they realised that Montague Smith could provide the customer with a much quicker and more personal service than they could offer. Which all helped our turnover, naturally, and increased our efficiency, so everybody gained.

## Cash Flow

So you might think that everything in the garden was lovely, as somebody has said. But that would be against the nature of things. We were offering the right goods, admittedly. And we were getting the orders. So where was the snag? In two words: cash flow. Even I can understand that it is no good selling stuff to a man who either never pays for it, or else who takes so long to produce the money that your own bank charges have absorbed the profit. But the boatbuilding industry had a long tradition of slow payment, not unlike that of the tailoring trade. A man would order a boat, browbeat the builder while she was taking shape and, as like as not, have a season's sailing before he finally settled his account– even then he would often still owe his sailmaker. In the circumstances it was hardly surprising that the likes of Montague Smith had to wait for their money like everyone else. But increasing business meant that we had to put more money into stock, so we had to get it from the builders more quickly. It took quite a long time to wean them from their ways, for they in turn had to get the money from their customers earlier. I often called on builders to find them with a row of half a dozen boats in various stages of completion, yet they would only order one pulpit and pushpit and one set of stanchions for the boat most nearly ready. Even the attraction of quantity discount failed to move them from the instincts of a lifetime, until eventually they too became more strict at enforcing stage payments from the owners, so that the whole chain of movement of money flowed more evenly; with attendant lowering of prices, I might add.

So, with the expansion of business caused by fibreglass production, the supplier could no longer afford to subsidise the owner–for that is how it had been. We stopped being a race apart, and became as other men; we demanded payment in thirty days or we withheld supplies.

Of course, we could not have taken this stand if there had been other suppliers ready to jump into our place with an equal service. But this is where our exclusive Lewmar agency and our policy of good after-sales service, coupled with the way our suppliers placed their confidence in us (in theory, Lewmar could have granted their agency to another company, more prepared to take an easy line over bills), paid off. The builders and chandlers wanted the goods, and they were also often glad to have someone call to discuss their requirements, from winch siting to halyard layout, and this is where my fairly wide experience came in useful. Like Olin Stephens, Ron Holland and other progressive designers, I made it my business to get around, sail in different boats, meet people, and it proved invaluable. So, when we demanded payment in thirty days, instead of the six months' grace which used to be the rule, the builders in turn had to chase their customers.

I suppose it was fortunate that a new generation was coming into sailing at that time. They had been brought up in a more commercial world and, instead of considering that they were conferring a favour in placing an order, they realised that they were engaging in a business transaction–in which, indeed, they were the customer with all the privileges which that implies, but in which they also had certain liabilities which had to be met. Builders started getting better stage payments, their cash flow problems eased so that they could order in advance, thus lessening the possibilities of delays due to shortages, and the wholesalers were able to stock up and give a better service. Once again, everybody gained, though there may be some who would say that the owner lost out. But he was only being asked to pay for goods he had bought and was using, and the final result was better service to him and his successors. Cash flow helps everybody except, perhaps, the man who has to start the flow; but it is usually he who benefits from greater efficiency in the end.

I had been grappling with the affairs of state for a couple of years on my own when it became obvious that, like Chippy Davy before me, I needed a number two. I am against taking on a man just because he is the son or brother of the foreman or sales manager so, when my own son (who I had unsuccessfully tried to persuade into the sailing industry when he left school–he'd been a tailor among other things, would you believe?) asked me about the chances of a job, I gave him the cold shoulder. Somebody must have mentioned it to the Ryland brothers, because they expressed their firm support for family connections in a business, and suggested that I should give him a try. The result is that he now works for me, filling roughly the slot I was in when I first joined Chippy Davy. I warned him at the start that it would be hard and that he would get no favours from me.

It is never easy to admit you have been wrong, but the pill tends to be sugared when it is your own kith and kin who is doing well against your forecast. The Ryland brothers were right, because Terry has done well, and you may be sure that he has been judged against a harder yardstick than any other employee would have encountered. I am now glad to record that he works for me, and it would take a lot to make me fire him (I hope he doesn't read this). He is lucky in that he does not have to shoulder the task of running the business while I am away, because my secretary has been with the firm only a year less than I have, so that she knows as much, if not more, about the office as I do.

### Diversification

One of the problems facing any company such as ours is the danger of putting all the eggs in one basket. It is all too easy to become over-dependent on one particular line which, in our case, could have proved to be Lewmar. Fortunately their products gave no cause for alarm, so their continuity was assured; nevertheless, it would have been unwise to rely on them too much. We were pretty busy with a number of other firms, but this in no way formed a spread of products sufficient to carry us through any trouble, and I would have been silly to have ignored it.

Once again fortune seemed to smile on us. Lewmar decided to drop one or two of their slower moving lines, for much the same reasons that we had earlier given up those products which we had felt to be slow moving as far as we were concerned. But what Lewmar looked upon as slow moving was still pretty big time for us so, with their approval, we arranged to take on the lines as they were dropped. In the end we had our own designs and dies, and were marketing Montague Smith exclusive products made in the midlands specially for us.

Since then we have moved still further. A couple of friends of mine started up System Fabrications recently, a business formed to manufacture metal products for the yachting industry. They were kind enough to ask me to join them in an advisory capacity, which my bosses gladly gave their consent for me to do. The new firm now makes, for the trade, those items like pulpits, pushpits and chain plates which Lewmar had given up, and which Montague Smith feel would be extending their range too much.

Finally, we have recently obtained the agency for the Camper & Nicholson range of fittings, such as hatches, vents, winch handle pockets and so on, which are marketed by their subsidiary Canpa.

So Montague Smith now have four principal sources of supply: our own directly manufactured goods, Lewmar, Canpa and System Fabrications, besides several smaller firms. Our turnover has increased some forty-fold from that £30,000 when I first joined the firm, and we have moved from our original rented premises to fine quarters in one of the 18th century squares in Southampton. You might think that we have made it, and you would not be very far wrong but, once again, it has not been quite as easy as it looks when written down in a few lines.

No firm can climb to the top of its own particular tree by staying still. In our case we had not only been active in seeking outlets, but had also built up a pretty good after-sales service which made customers come back to us with repeat orders; we have proved that it is good business to pay more than lip service to the maxim that the customer is always right. As I have already said, we had a good line of products during a period of active expansion in the whole yachting industry, and we made it our business to co-operate with our suppliers in improving their products and in evolving new items. This was particularly the case with Lewmar and then, of course, later on we were able to develop the Montague Smith range, followed by that of System Fabrications.

### Development of Equipment

My involvement with *Kurrewa* enabled us to take an active interest in all her gear. Lewmar people were on the boat almost more than we were, as they tested winches and developed their new mainsheet traveller. Mr Aisher was very good in all this for, if we thought we were on to a good thing, he gave us every encouragement. Out of it all came the Lewmar X section mainsheet traveller, working on stainless steel rollers (the Proctor recirculating ballrace traveller also appeared at this time), together with their genoa sliders and improved snap shackles. In the end the two British twelves were equipped with some very good gear, all more or less one-off fabrications, but the ordinary racing and cruising man profited from it because these improvements eventually led to standard production items for the benefit of all. Of course, when we came back from America in 1964 we brought a lot of new ideas with us, much the same as Mr Millar and I did for Avica when we had raced for a season in *Palawan* eight years earlier. So it all moved rapidly ahead.

Later, when Mr Heath was having the second *Morning Cloud* built by Lallows at Cowes, Lewmar proposed the idea of linking the sheet winches to a common drive. I put this to Mr Heath who, as usual, was flat out for anything which might prove useful and where we could be the first to have it. Lewmar were glad to have a keen boat in good hands on which to do the development work.

Fig 8. The full pedestal
links winches on either
side of the boat under
the cockpit floor.
*Courtesy: Lewmar*

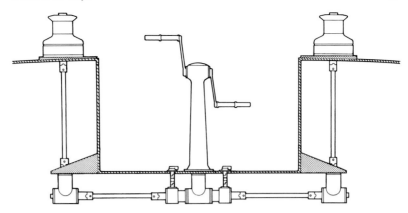

They also knew that there were certain to be teething troubles, but that I wouldn't cry too much if things went wrong.

The basic idea behind linked winches, as most people know these days, is to enable two handles to be turned when real power is wanted at, say, a genoa sheet. Equally, when on a reach, it is possible to wind the windward handle and thereby turn the winch down to leeward, thus keeping weight from the wrong side of the boat. You had to slip cones in and out of mesh to engage and disengage the double drive. We tried them first of all on winch pads built up clear of the coaming. Then, because the leverage on the six inch pads was too great, we dropped them below the coaming onto the bridge deck. Even then, the strain on a winch is pretty hefty at the best of times, and doubling the muscle power soon had the effect of shifting the whole apparatus–bridge deck and all. This had to be reinforced, the cones had to be improved and several mountings and bearings needed altering, but when it was working it was fantastic.

Handle sockets away from the winch itself–molehills–were introduced, and nowadays the whole affair comes in a lightweight alloy box which is dropped into place, and there you have the package deal: three-speed winches, linkage, clutch, winding–the lot.

Not everybody was sold on the idea in the early stages. There was a natural tendency to look across the Atlantic, and the

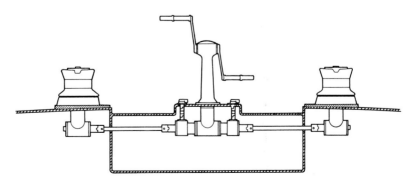

Fig 9. The mini-pedestal
system which has been
developed to link
winches via the bridge
deck. *Courtesy: Lewmar*

Americans were using more coffee grinders than we were. This, of course, is a form of linked system, but they did not think that Lewmar's idea would be needed on the smaller boats which had no call for a coffee grinder. When we showed how to use it to such good effect in *Morning Cloud*, people over in England started clamouring for it, and soon the Americans realised that they had to get on the band waggon. It had an obvious application for the smaller boats as well as the big boys, so there had to be a future in it.

Coming nearer to the present, lever jammers had a swift explosion around 1975, when a number of Admiral's Cup boats used them. The idea at the time was to do away with the battery of winches which seemed to be essential round the mast, and Ron Holland among others used a single winch each side of the mast, backed up by a cluster of lever jammers. The halyard would be wound up, jammed, and taken off the winch, which was then free to be used again. But slowly the winches started reappearing as crews found that the jammers were rather inconvenient in this role, and were also chewing up the halyards themselves. I bought 250 from New Zealand that year, and they all went quickly, but we have never had many re-orders. They are OK acting as relievers for genoa sheets, and also on the spinnaker sheet if you suddenly need to switch it to the genoa winch in order to get the faster winding conferred by the pedestal or coffee grinder, but they proved to be a bit of a flash in the pan as regards taking the place of halyard winches.

To sum up, therefore, although our business has remained substantially the same since I joined Chippy Davy back in 1961, in that we supply paint, fixtures and fittings for yachts, the structure of the Company has changed. We no longer supply direct to the public, but concentrate on production builders, designers and chandleries, in that order of turnover per customer. We have streamlined the list of our suppliers by cutting out the slow moving lines and small manufacturers, but have added to the range by taking on some others, thereby avoiding the danger of over-dependence on one supplier. Above all, we maintain personal contact with our customers and give them advice over deck layout if they want it, good delivery, back-up service and after-sales care. We have a good accountant, who sees to it that we keep up the pressure for prompt payment, thus easing the cash flow.

I like my job because I like my customers and my suppliers; it is nice to think that this is a two way appreciation. No man could ask for more understanding bosses than the Ryland brothers, who have done me the honour of making me a director of Montague Smith. Although I am also the manager, I have always felt that the title Managing Director smacks too much of the board room and not enough of the sweat shop, so I still call myself the manager. The chaps in the firm didn't think I knew about it when they first started to call me the Guv'nor, but they couldn't have given me any name I'd like better, and they call me that to my face now.

# five The Sydney-Hobart

When I came back from America, I went back to sailing with Guy Bowles. By now *Sunmaid IV* was well into her stride and we had five marvellous seasons in her. All this time I was working for Montague Smith at Southampton and helping to build up the business, as I have already related. This, perhaps, was a period of consolidation, when I built on the formative years of my life, helped by the wonderful spirit of trust and co-operation which developed between Mr Bowles and myself. I have already mentioned his qualities as a helmsman, and I would like here to pay my tribute to him as a friend; he trusted me and for my part I tried never to let him down.

By the year 1969 Montague Smith was doing good business world wide. We had the agency for Lewmar Marine, which was a good thing for the Company, because their winches were second to none–partly, I may say, due to the readiness with which they co-operated with users who could point the way to improvement and development. Certainly Chippy Davy and I were able to put across some ideas and, as we have seen, some of these were successfully tried out on the various *Morning Clouds*.

## Morning Cloud

As most people know, Mr Heath came to ocean racing from dinghies–Snipes and Fireballs as it happens. The first *Morning Cloud* was the result of a visit to the London Boat Show, where Mr Heath looked at a lot of boats, liked the Sparkman & Stephens 34 and happened to meet the designer Olin Stephens on the stand, and finished up buying one. She was launched at Rochester in April 1969 and, as Montague Smith had supplied most of the deck fittings, I was kindly asked along. On the back of my invitation card were the words 'Bring your sailing gear.'

We went out in her on the Saturday for a shake-down, and generally tuned and tried her. At the end of the day Mr Heath asked me whether I would like to sail with him that season, an honour which I had to turn down because I was committed to Guy Bowles.

*Morning Cloud* sailed with a certain amount of success that year, and Mr Heath declared his intention of going in for the Sydney–Hobart race; this starts on 26th December, so fits in well

Fig. 10. Olin Stephens, designer of the first four *Morning Clouds*, at the wheel of Dennis Miller's *Firebrand*. She has two roller bearing mainsheet travellers developed by Lewmar for the 1964 America's Cup challenge. *Photo: Lewmar*

with the Parliamentary recess. The boat had not, unfortunately, done well enough to make the British team for the Southern Cross series, but she was selected to travel as reserve. Another S & S 34, *Morning After*, was the third boat and, on their respective showings in the Solent, she deserved her place.

Towards the end of the season Mr Bowles laid *Sunmaid* up, leaving me free to accept an invitation from Mr Heath to join him for the second half of Burnham week. I arrived to find a rare old discussion going on among the crew, as they suggested all sorts of wild and impractical ideas for improving on their somewhat disappointing performance over the last couple of days. Morale was not high and people were finding fault with the sails, the design, the keel, the sailplan, the rating–you name it, they blamed it, in a see-sawing criticism which swayed back and forth across the full range of possible culprits. I sat listening to this for a long time, trying to sound non-committal when appealed to by one or other of the crew, until I could stand it no longer.

'Look, sir,' I said. 'You've got the bloody boat as she is, you'd best get on and bloody well sail her as she is.'

As it happened, this was just the advice they needed. I claim no great credit for producing it at the right moment, because there was clearly no time to do anything drastic before the next day's racing, but it was patently obvious that something needed to be done for morale. When they asked me my opinion, I merely stated what was obvious to me as a newcomer to the team. So we got on with sailing her, and as soon as we had done well in our next race (we came second), all talk of altering the boat was forgotten and we went from strength to strength.

I must confess at this stage that I nearly put the lid on it right away. Trying to get a really good start I overdid it and arrived at the line three or four seconds early, so we were over and had to work our way back.

'Sorry sir,' I said, and really meant it.

'Never mind,' replied the Skipper. 'But don't do it too often.'

But everybody minds this sort of thing. I mind, and it stayed with me for a while. But you cannot let yourself dwell on these things, and have to get down to the race again quickly. Anyway, the man who is never over never starts consistently well–you have got to get up on the line and be right there, so obviously you will misjudge it from time to time. But I could have wished that I hadn't chosen an early race to try it in this instance.

## Australia

At the end of the week Mr Heath asked me to join the crew on their Australian trip. Now, all the others were paying their own way, but this was quite beyond my pocket and I told Mr Heath so, thus presenting him with a nice problem. The *Cloud* was a democratic boat, so how could he pay for one crew member and not all the

others? He answered in the true democratic manner, as subsequent experience showed was his routine aboard. The crew were
told the problem and asked to decide whether an exception could
and should be made. They seemed to think that I could help them,
because they unanimously decided that I should come.

So I joined Sammy Sampson, an Essex farmer who was 45 then
and had been in the Royal Navy in World War II; he was a born
helmsman. The navigator was Anthony Churchill, a journalist
who has been ocean racing since the early sixties and was a wizard
with charts and compass. We also had a Swiss business man who
had lived in England for a dozen years or so: Jean Berger, who
graduated with honours from Hornet dinghies to winning the
RORC Class II in 1966, when he moved into the One-Ton class—he
was second relief helmsman. Duncan Kay, aged 30, made up the
crew; he had sailed for over 20 years and would share the foredeck
work with me. As I also take the tiller on occasions, it will be
noticed that, with the owner, we had four helmsmen on board—a
fact which helped considerably as will be seen later.

Some of this crew called the owner 'Edward' and one or two of
the later members such as Peter Nicholson called him 'Ted', but
this is not my way. You will have seen that I was brought up in the
old school, so I always called my customers 'sir'. Mr Heath was a
customer, and I treated him accordingly. On board, I found it
natural to continue out of respect for him, and it has never been
anything other than 'sir', 'Mr Heath' or 'Skipper'; if he asked me to
use his christian name, I think we'd both find it awkward. In fact,
I've never been on christian name terms with any of my owners—as
a professional before 1959, of course, it had to be 'sir'; after I
returned to amateur status, I was still a semi-professional sailing
at someone else's expense, so the courtesy remained.

The Sydney–Hobart is one of the world's three classic offshore
races—the round the world and trans-ocean races are something
apart, for not many people can spare the time to take part in such
marathons. The other two, of course, are the Fastnet and the
Bermuda races. It was in the Bugle Inn at Hamble, after a
successful day's racing on the Solent, that Mr Heath first had the
idea that he might like to have a go at the Sydney–Hobart. It is the
culmination of the Southern Cross series, and teams of three boats
may be entered by each country; as it is rather a long way for
anybody to cart three ocean racers, the amount of entries tends to
be small, so each Australian state may enter a team to keep up
numbers and interest. Even though we were not in the official
British team, there was a lot of planning to do, and it was
interesting to see how an expert set about it.

**Planning**

Mr Heath used to get us together in his flat in Albany, off
Piccadilly. We'd go there to breakfast, so as to thrash out our
problems before the Skipper had to dash off to his parliamentary

duties as Leader of Her Majesty's Opposition. We'd all sit round eating and talking while Mr Heath leaned back and soaked it all up. Then, suddenly, he'd make a decision and we would go on to the next point. I've never been much of a one for paper work, but some of the others would write pages and pages on some points; when it came to me, like as not I hadn't had the patience to read it all, so I'd have to tag along as best I could. I'm better at decisions on board, where you haven't time to put it all down in writing because, if you don't do something damn quick, you'll gybe all standing.

I do remember that one of our big debates was what to do with the rating we saved by fitting stringers round the inside of the hull (this was a stratagem whereby the hull was strengthened and you reduced the rating due to a clause in the rule–don't ask me to explain exactly how it worked). There were those who favoured taking the lower rating and being grateful, while the other camp wanted to get back to our original handicap by adding to the sail area–bigger headsails and spinnakers, in fact. I couldn't follow the closely typed memos which were flying back and forth, but it made sense to take more area if there was less weight in the wind and if you could carry it, and I said so. In the end we had bigger sails made, and very glad of them we were too.

One final point was decided by Mr Heath, without any discussion. When he had been on the Fastnet race, he had run his batteries dry using the radio telephone daily to keep in touch with politics. This time we would carry a second bank of batteries.

## The Big One

The crew flew out during the first week in December. We stopped off for 24 hours in Hong Kong, that wonderful island where East meets West against a background of oriental mystery. We had dinner in the famous Tai-Pak restaurant, floating in the middle of the harbour and surrounded by the junks, smells, noise, neon lights and guttering lanterns which go to make up an unforgettable experience–at least, it was unforgettable for the Hampshire lad who had started life in another, and quite different, international port. I was naïve enough to have packed my swimming trunks for this break in our journey, quite forgetting that Hong Kong is well north of the equator and thus was still in the middle of winter.

When we arrived in Sydney we found the boat waiting for us, and went straight along to set her up. Mr Heath was not able to spare the time for the first two races, and was to join us for one inshore race and then the big one; in the event, one of the earlier races had to be re-sailed after he arrived, so the Skipper was lucky. There was no warming up period, and our first race was the first in the Southern Cross series, from which we went straight into the medium long one of 200 miles. Our team consisted of team captain Arthur Slater's *Prospect of Whitby*, Sir Max Aitken's big *Crusade* and Rodney Hill's *Morning After*, and none of the British boats, us included, did particularly well to start with–it would have been surprising if we had, with so little time to get acclimatised. The Australians treated us marvellously, and each boat had someone assigned to her to see that she had everything she wanted. This included tips and hints on local waters, the rather special conditions to be expected during the Sydney–Hobart itself, or such matters as laundry, beer and mail from home. In addition Trygve Halvorsen, an Australian who had Norwegian ancestry, and who had sailed the big race several times and was going this time as navigator on Alan Bond's *Apollo*, also helped out with advice. He it was who recommended that we smooth off the toggle on our forestay fitting and pack it with grease, to ease the chafe and wear as it worked in the heavy local swell. I can't say I was glad to hear this, as we'd just got the rigging set up and tuned, and it meant taking it all to pieces again; but we did it and it was good advice.

Much had been made of the southerly set which you might encounter if you got far enough east of the rhumb line, and you could expect an increase in water temperatures of 3–4 degrees and to meet jellyfish as soon as you got into this set. Most Australian boats had through-hull thermometers so that they could see what was happening, but we had to fall back on gathering buckets of water every two or three hours and checking the temperature from these. I can't say that we ever found the dramatic change from 68–72 degrees which we were looking for, but it gave an interest to the day and we would bombard the navigator with questions as he went through his almost religious dipping ritual, for all the world as though he could produce another knot of speed from a bucketful of water.

The disadvantage of going east of the rhumb line, of course, was that by doing so you would sail a greater distance than necessary. The nice calculation arose as to the amount you could afford to stray from the shortest route in search of this elusive and obviously important southerly set. Would it be there? How far east would it lie? How fast would it be? Even if you found it, would the wind (usually a following one for the first part of the course) be a good one over there, and how about when it came ahead for the final part of the race as it usually did, would it come dead ahead or would you be able to lay the line? Finally there was some doubt, even among the Australians, as to the nature of the set, and not everyone was agreed that it would necessarily be southerly; there were those who claimed that it might go the other way–it all depended on recent weather conditions. Indeed, we learned later that *Crusade* and *Apollo* had fought a duel pretty well on the rhumb line, hoping to profit from the shorter distance. So you see that there were a lot of factors which had to be weighed when the decision was being made as to the strategy for the race.

The first three races in the series had put our colleagues in the British team in a reasonable place overall, without being anything to write home about. The conditions were new to all of us, so they had reason to be happy with an average performance. The Sydney–

Hobart itself was started at 11 o'clock on the morning of Boxing Day 1969 by Mr John Gorton, the Australian Prime Minister. There were 79 starters, the biggest field yet, ranging from just over 30 ft to 70 ft overall, of which *Morning After* and ourselves were among the smallest, and there were boats from America, France, Japan and New Zealand as well as Britain and the various states of Australia. It was a windward start and I remember the impressive sight made by the 12-metre *American Eagle* as she sliced her way through the water, dwarfing and outdistancing the rest of the fleet. 'They'll have a wet ride' I thought, looking at her fine entry and low freeboard without the protection of a decent doghouse. Thousands of onlookers crowded the shores and pressed in on us in spectator craft. The latter were, however, highly disciplined and never got in the way of the racing yachts as we beat to windward towards the Heads and open water in a kindly force 3. Once outside, the wind went into the north and there began the most wonderful downhill slide which lasted over two and a half days. Up went the spinnaker and away we went. We had all agreed that we would go east in search of the set, for a 2-knot current favours big and small alike and, because of handicap, the small boats profit most, unlike a stronger wind which often only helps the bigger yachts, because it enables them to reach their maximum hull speed, whereas the smaller boats are already going as fast as they can. We got onto the port gybe and sailed her at 15–20 degrees to the dead run, which carried us over the rhumb line and away east, dipping our bucket regularly into the water and the thermometer as regularly into the bucket.

After some time the navigator rather felt that we were edging too far across, so we gybed over and made a short board back towards the rhumb line. But it was obvious that the other gybe was the paying one, so off we went again on port tack which carried us east again. All this time the wind was blowing from the north quadrant at something between force 4–6. It was warm by day and night, and I learned the meaning of the word 'sleighride' when applied to sailing. There was not the weight to the wind that there usually is in England, so we never needed to shorten canvas–in fact we were glad of our bigger headsails and kept the same spinnaker up for over 60 hours as we bowled along at a steady 6 knots.

At no time were we worried that we were getting too far away from the best line, because our course always seemed good and the wind was nudging us to the east; yet we never struck a sharp rise in water temperature, so we couldn't have been too far over. Everything felt just right.

But it did not last like this the whole way. The last part of the course always brings a beat to windward as the wind goes into the south and gets heavier. And my goodness, how the air temperature drops. From lolling about under the warm sun, we switched to thrashing to windward in a heavy antarctic wind with cold spray everywhere. Suddenly we were in oilskins and, to make matters worse, the boat was making quite a lot of water. To cap it all, the

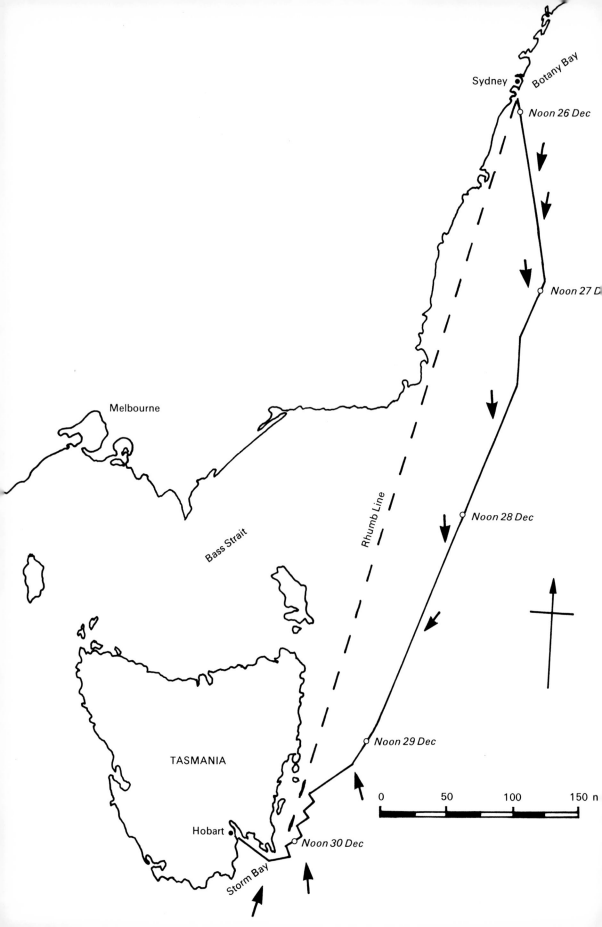

bilge pump wouldn't work, the galley packed up and we developed a diesel leak.

We set about trying to trace the water leak without success. The most obvious places in any boat are the stern gland and the deck/hull joint on a fibreglass boat or the deck itself if she is made of wood. These seemed all right so there was nothing for it but to get down to baling by hand. We all took it in turns, skipper and crew alike, and it was no joke reefed down, lying on our ear with the stench of diesel, and water coming into the cockpit in great waves from time to time, to undo all the work you had just done.

In the most important point, however, we had been lucky. We knew from the positions which every boat had to give regularly over the radio that we were further to the east than anybody, and it didn't take much working out that a sou-westerly wind would put us right down to leeward of everybody and poorly placed. It is always a bit of a toss-up as to where the southerly wind will fill in from, and we had to pray that there wouldn't be too much west in it. In the event it came in from just east of south so, despite our extra work and loss of sleep due to baling, at least we had the wind we wanted. There was more than enough of it, as I have described, and the inside of the boat became a shambles. The crew off watch could not get up to windward to sleep, and we threw a couple of sailbags down to leeward so that we were not actually lying in the pools of water which were sloshing everywhere, and slept in our wet oilskins.

## The Finish

After a while this sort of life begins to get a bit tiresome, and just a little of the edge went out of us. That is, until Anthony announced that he reckoned we were fairly well placed. Mr Heath then showed some of his qualities as a leader, for nothing was too much effort for him as he encouraged us to greater efforts by his own example. We trimmed sails, baled, worked to windward, baled, tightened the backstay a bit more as the wind got even stronger, baled and fought our way up to windward. All this in a welter of wet gear, leaking diesel oil, cooking gas fumes and a fairly rough sea.

'Things can only get better,' said the Skipper, pausing to wipe salt spray from his face as he chucked yet another bucketful of water over the side. 'Keep her going Sammy, we'll get there one day.'

Now the presence of four helmsmen really paid off. We were all physically tired, and long spells on the tiller were not advisable; the heavy antarctic winds of 35–40 knots made conditions so cold that half an hour on deck was about all we could stand. We cut the watch to two men and switched duties fairly often, each man striving to do better than his predecessor. Sammy Sampson and Jean Berger were the mainstays of this effort, for they were the

Fig 12. The finish of the Sydney–Hobart. Jean Berger and Sammy Sampson are involved in a twin pole gybe, while I am chain smoking down below.

most experienced helmsmen, but Mr Heath and I were able to take a turn in order to give them time to relax–if you can call baling relaxation.

Most people know that it is important to have a tight forestay when going to windward, but our genoa luff seemed to sag away in the fresh conditions and lumpy sea rather more than we thought right. We had a Camper & Nicholson hydraulic backstay adjuster, so we pumped away to harden it down and pull the forestay tight. It seemed to work for a while, and then the sag reappeared, so we pumped down on the backstay again. This went on for 24 hours until Tasmania hove in sight, looking eerily bleak and inhospitable through the driving spray. We had twenty miles to do across Storm Bay–a name to fit in with the sense of occasion–before we would reach the shelter of the river Derwent and a further ten miles to the finishing line. Just after entering Storm Bay we heard the first radio reports that not only were we fairly well up, but we stood a chance of overall honours–we had to finish by six o'clock to do it. We were lucky, for though the wind had veered 20 degrees or more, we were able to set the spinnaker, genoa, staysail and full mainsail, as the wind took off slightly and gave us a spanking reach, so that we crossed the bay with all the washing up in just over two and a half hours to average nearly 8 knots. From the mouth of the river to the finish there are hills on either side which can cause the wind to be a little fluky. We arrived at the entry with time to spare and our hopes high.

Then the wind went dead astern and dropped almost to nothing, so that we were hardly moving through the water.

Slowly we inched our way forward, until we could see the finishing line a mile ahead. We were now on a dead run, and what wind there was swung further so that we were running by the lee and still getting in under the headland. I couldn't stand the tension any longer.

'For chrissake gybe,' I croaked as I turned to go below for a cigarette. 'We'll be becalmed under the lee of the land in a minute and never get there in time to save our time.'

With that I disappeared to chain smoke, my nerves in shreds, unable to watch, let alone take any further active part.

From the activity on deck it was obvious that we were, indeed, gybing. What's more it was Jean Berger and Sammy Sampson who were kindly exploring new territory for them and getting forward of the mast to do Duncan's and my job for us. It may not have been the best gybe that was ever done, but it was effective and, with 250 yards to go, we pulled away from the wind shadow and ghosted across the line.

Then all hell broke loose.

Every hooter, siren, gong and foghorn in the place started up such a racket as you have never heard. Grins all round on board, of course, and I've never before or since seen Mr Heath so excited.

'Start the engine,' he called when we had stopped chattering. But this was easier said than done, and it flatly refused to go, so we had to take a tow. But we didn't care, everything pointed to a resounding victory, and that's what we had come for.

When all the points were added up, the British Southern Cross team came second to one of the Australian states. *Prospect of Whitby* came second in the Sydney–Hobart and contributed a lot of points, but none of *Morning Cloud*'s points counted, of course, because we had not been in the team; the British yachting correspondents were quick to note however that, if we had been the third member instead of *Morning After*, Britain would have taken the trophy by a handsome margin. But that's sailing for you– *Morning After* thoroughly deserved her place on our respective showings before the selection, and we only started to come good after the team had been decided.

Among the festivities was an invitation to Government House. In common with his invariable practice, whenever he was invited anywhere Mr Heath always replied 'There's six of us you know,' and we went everywhere as a crew. Anyway, this was obviously a fairly formal occasion, so we had to dig out our dark suits from the luggage which had been flown down ahead of us.

'Guess whose is the only suitcase missing,' grinned Mr Heath when Trygve Halvorsen had come aboard to tell us where they all were. So off we went with the crew smartly dressed in suits and the Skipper in sailing trousers and a salt stained sweater.

Tryg was as pleased that 'his' boat had won as if *Apollo* herself had done it–more so, I think, and he couldn't do enough for us. Sadly anticlimax quickly set in, because Mr Heath had to get back to politics and we had to pack up the boat and return to England ourselves, but not before we were able to sample some wonderful Tasmanian hospitality and to find out that their beautiful country belies the rather bleak impression we had gained on first sighting it during the race; we also had the thrill of making an appearance on Australian television.

When we got the boat out of the water, we found that our leak had been coming through the cockpit lockers, which were later satisfactorily modified when we got back to England; we also found that we had been making some water through the keelbolts, which had understandably worked a little in the pounding they had received. What is more, the extra tension we kept putting on the backstay had bent the clevis pin of the forestay toggle, so that I had to drive it out with a hammer. Another day of that and we might easily have lost our mast. I think that the repeated slackening of the forestay can only be put down to the fact that we were pulling the ends of the boat upwards in our hydraulically assisted exertions.

When the time came to analyse our victory, we could point to a number of factors which had been important. First, the navigator had done his homework properly and had planned his strategy to take full advantage of the set, which he correctly assessed would be favourable, and reckoning from the long range weather forecast that the wind on the second part of the course would not play us false. Throughout the bruising final 24 hours Anthony kept a good plot of our position under conditions which cannot have been easy for good chart work; it was vital not to make a mistake at that time and he didn't let us down.

Secondly, we were lucky to have on board four people who could take the helm. Sailing down wind is taxing offshore, and we were able to spell each other at regular intervals. When it came to the final thrash to the finish, Jean Berger and Sammy Sampson rose to the occasion and dragged up powers of concentration from some hidden reserves, with help from the Skipper and myself.

Thirdly, Mr Heath's leadership was superb. There was a lot of experience on board and he wisely let us get on with it, taking his full part in the sailing, encouraging by example and keeping our spirits up. Nothing was too much for him, and he was quite content to take more than his share of the most arduous jobs. The team spirit engendered ashore certainly paid off during the final slog to windward.

I haven't said anything about my old mate Duncan Kay. He was a tower of strength on the foredeck and, having raced for the whole of 1969 in the boat, he knew her better than I. There was nothing he would not do if called upon, and we got on well together, so we knew that sail drills would not let us down.

Finally, Tryg Halvorsen had been very helpful. Apart from discussing the important set *ad nauseam*, he gave us one other piece of advice which stood out among his many tips and hints.

'If you need to change down jibs,' he said, 'don't take half measures. If it's going to blow harder, it'll really hit you, so always change two sizes not one. If you've got a number one genny on, change to a number three and leave the intermediate in the locker. Same goes for changing up.'

* * *

On the way home by air, Duncan, Jean and I stopped off in Singapore. On my bed in the hotel that evening I found an envelope on which was written 'We couldn't have done it without you.'

Inside was one-third of the winnings which they had collected for a bet they had placed on us at 33:1 before the start. I was very touched at this generous gesture, and believe me we had fun spending it together.

# six The Admiral's Cup

The Admiral's Cup is competed for in a series of races organised by
the Royal Ocean Racing Club in British waters, every alternate
year to coincide with the Fastnet race, which culminates the
series. The trophy is therefore contested in odd years, and this is
arranged so as not to conflict with the similar Onion Patch series
which is staged in America in even years, finishing with the
Bermuda Race; the Onion Patch is the name by which Americans
affectionately know the British island 500 miles off their eastern
seaboard. Countries enter teams of three boats, and the Admiral's
Cup, which was only started in 1957, has quickly become the major
trophy as far as the British ocean racing man is concerned, if not
the European and American; the honour of making the national
team is highly coveted, with owners building boats specially
designed to catch the selectors' eye.

**Candidate for the Team**

After we had done so well in the Sydney–Hobart race, the germ
formed in Mr Heath's mind that he would like to try for the
Admiral's Cup team. The crew had a number of meetings to discuss
this early in 1970, so we all knew what was happening, and so that
each could decide whether he could give up the not inconsiderable
time next year which the preliminary trial races, followed by the
series itself, would take if we were to be selected. At 34 ft overall,
*Morning Cloud* was too small to be eligible for the team (which has
to be made up of boats within certain rated sizes, the dimensions of
which vary occasionally, but which are generally fairly large), so
it was obvious that we would have to have a new boat.

The first *Cloud* had been a production boat with a fibreglass hull
and deck of a standard Sparkman & Stephens design–the so-called
S & S 34. This time it was decided that we would have a one-off boat
specially designed, and built in wood. I know that Mr Heath would
have preferred to go to a British designer for this commission, but
two factors weighed heavily against this. First, at that time the
Stephens brothers were by far the most successful designers for the
type of boat he had in mind, standing head and shoulders clear of
anyone else. Secondly, he had formed a close working relationship
with Olin Stephens following the purchase of the first *Morning
Cloud* from Mike Winfield. Their first meeting on the Winfield

stand at the London Boat Show was one of those encounters where Fate might or might not have been given a helping hand. To all intents and purposes Olin was on the stand where the S & S 34 was being displayed, entirely by chance when Mr Heath came along to see the boat again, after a previous tour of the Show when he had been round the entire hall. Few people knew that he was to make a return visit, but Mike Winfield was certainly one of them, though he probably did not know the exact time. Now, Olin Stephens was not the sort of man to hang around all day waiting for a meeting, so we can certainly give Dame Fortune some, if not all, of the credit for the happy coincidence. At all events, from this encounter grew an excellent business association, which was fostered as we got the boat ready for the Southern Cross series in Australia, when Olin was of particular help in advising on modifications to take advantage of the rule by putting stringers round the inside of the hull.

So it was decided quite early in 1970 that we would go to Sparkman & Stephens for the design, and that she would be built in wood. There was a lot of sense in choosing a builder on the south coast, because a number of the crew lived in the area and would be able to watch her progress. Moodys, Camper & Nicholson and Lallows were all obvious candidates and Mr Heath finally chose Lallows in Cowes, partly because it was hoped that Ian Lallow, Clare's son, might be able to sail with us. I've got a funny feeling that it was me who first suggested Lallows for the job but, as usual, the whole crew had a say and Mr Heath then made the final choice.

Meanwhile *Morning Cloud* returned from her triumph on the other side of the world, and I went to Dunkirk to sail her back to the Hamble River. This proved to be a minor epic in itself. First, the mast had been lashed on deck for the trip, so I had to arrange for it to be stepped. The rigging was stowed properly, because we had done this ourselves in Tasmania, but there was no dockside crane which could do the job, so I had to set about hiring one. French is not my strong point, and I was mentally exhausted by the time the whole thing was over and done with. Then the weather took a hand. The temperature dropped and the wind went firmly into the west, so we had a beat for the whole trip, which must have established some sort of record for the longest ever Dunkirk–Solent. When we got home we were frozen stiff and I remember thinking 'If this is sailing, I'll give it up for good.'

We got her ready for the 1970 season, which was spent carefully observing every other successful boat we encountered. Each man was to have his say in the layout of the new boat, so we all determined to be in a position to know what was the latest thinking as regards our own particular area. This was also a period for selecting additional crew members, because the new boat would require more people to run her and, in addition, Jean Berger had to drop out because of business commitments. We tried a number of good men and eventually suggested a list of names to Mr Heath, with their specialities noted and our own thoughts on each one. The Skipper chose George Stead as a helmsman to replace Jean Berger, Pete Dove from Hood's UK sail loft as a useful midshipman (apart from his keenness and ability as a crew, we had a full suit of Hood sails, and he was able to see to it that we got good service and delivery). The newcomers were completed by Peter Holt, who had sailed with me in the *Sunmaids*, to work on the foredeck with Duncan Kay. This left me free to come into the cockpit as sailing master and tactician, joining Sammy Sampson (helm), Anthony Churchill (navigator), and Mr Heath (skipper/helm).

## The Onion Patch

At the beginning of the season, Lloyds Yacht Club had invited Anthony Churchill and myself to join the crew of their club boat *Lutine*, a Nicholson 55, which was going to America to race in the Onion Patch series as one of the British team; the other boats were to be *Prospect of Whitby II*, our old rival and British team captain in the recent Southern Cross series in Australia (and it was nice to find Ian Lallow and Wally Smythers aboard), and *Cervantes*. Mr Heath was in full agreement that we should go, not only so that we might bring back ideas for the new boat from the other top ocean racers we would see, but also to get experience of the Bermuda Race, which might one day come in useful. The series was to be sailed in June/July, so we would be away for little over a month and only miss one British offshore race of any importance.

The Onion Patch follows the usual pattern for this kind of competition, having one medium race of some 250 miles, three short inshore races and a high scoring long race–in this case the Newport–Bermuda. As a boat *Lutine* did reasonably well, but regretfully *Prospect* was damaged unloading, and never regained her previous fine tuning, so the British team as a whole was not too good. But we all thoroughly enjoyed ourselves in the customary American hospitality.

It so happened that Anthony Churchill, Ian Lallow and I were having dinner together in a Newport restaurant on the night when the results of the British parliamentary election came through– being five hours behind UK time, we were getting their midnight early indications at seven o'clock in the evening. I have never been a great political fanatic, but my association with Edward Heath gave me extra reason to support the Conservatives and wish him every success. To be quite honest, I don't think many of the *Morning Cloud* crew thought he would be returned to power, but we all hoped he would. We liked him as a man, as a skipper and as a friend, so we hoped he would succeed.

Half way through dinner an American reporter, knowing our association with the *Cloud*, came to our table and told us that the early results from the election indicated that Mr Heath looked to be doing very well. We stayed on, heard the eventual confirmation of his victory, ordered up a bottle of champagne and sent him a telegram:

CONGRATULATIONS ON ELECTION VICTORY STOP HERES TO
EVEN GREATER SUCCESS IN ELECTION TO ADMIRALS
CUP TEAM STOP ANTHONY AND OWEN

*Lutine*'s best performance was in the final long race to Bermuda, where we might have done even better but for an unusual incident. About half way through the race, we had *Palawan III* (another echo from my earlier racing in the USA; a later boat, she was owned by Thomas Watson's brother Arthur) in sight astern of us as dusk fell. This pleased us, because she was a 58-footer from the board of Sparkman & Stephens and had to give us quite a lot of time. We were close hauled on port tack in 20 knots of wind and had crossed *Palawan* by some distance as she went off the other way on starboard.

'Hey Owen,' called Peter Nicholson who was on the wheel. 'What do you make of that?'

He pointed ahead where, dimly in the fading light we could see a kind of white haze with what appeared to be choppy water under it. At that moment the wind dropped away to nothing, the boat came upright and we could hear an eerie rustling which gradually became louder till it roared in our ears.

'I'm damned if I know,' I replied, coming aft. 'But I'll take the mainsheet off the cleat so we'll be ready for anything.'

With that we were hit by a miniature whirlwind. The wind speed jumped from zero to 60 knots, the boat laid right over on her side, and I let the mainsheet run.

'Get the genny off her,' shouted Peter above the roar of wind and waves, as he struggled with the wheel. But it was too late and the wind did it for us, ripping the canvas to shreds. With the thrashing boom dragging in the water and gallons of the stuff pouring green into the cockpit, it was all we could do to hold on. Then, just as suddenly as it had started, it stopped and we came bolt upright in complete calm and quiet.

'The eye of the storm,' shouted someone. 'Get everything off her, it'll come again.'

The gooseneck had been shattered and the boom swung crazily at the end of the lifeless mainsail, the tattered remnants of the genoa hung from the forestay. We worked like demons to clear everything away, and by the time the force of the wind struck again we had all canvas off her and everything battened down, so were able to ride it out comfortably.

When it had passed we took stock of our situation. We would have to rig some kind of jury lashing for the main boom, and this would not only take time, it would certainly mean a poorer performance. Bang went our chances of achieving anything at all in the race.

'This any good to you?' asked someone, coming up from below. He was holding, of all things, a complete spare gooseneck, which some genius with second sight had thought fit to stow in the bilges before we were shipped from England. In ten minutes we had the new gooseneck fitted, the sails up and were under way again.

*Palawan III*, who knew these waters and must have seen the phenomenon approaching, had sailed right round it, along with our other principal rivals, and she beat us to Bermuda and saved her time by about an hour; she was fourth overall and we had to be content with fifth place. But racing is full of 'might-have-beens', and it was not to be our year.

Bermuda is a most beautiful island, with green grass and trees which remind you of England. The hospitality is wonderful and I was once again made to realise how lucky I have been. It all goes back to the hard work of my younger days, which fitted me to be some kind of an expert with marketable skills. It was great to see the IOD's racing again, for they still had quite a strong fleet out there in those days, and I was filled with nostalgia. Perhaps I'll retire there in my old age, find a rotting IOD and do her up for gentle picnics in the sun . . .

## The New Boat

So Anthony Churchill and I came back with our heads full of American ideas, backed up by rolls of film of all we had seen. We wanted to be able to think dispassionately, and to show the rest of the crew some of the layouts we had been looking at–all with a view to improving the new *Morning Cloud*.

Once again, although Mr Heath was paying for the new boat, we all looked on her as ours. She was, in fact, more 'our' boat than any I have ever sailed in, because we all put so much thought into her. As I have said, we looked at every other boat from a new angle, because we wanted to get the new one right. In the end, we virtually designed the deck layout ourselves, to the outline plan which Olin and Rod Stephens drew for us. The foredeck men said how they wanted the gear arranged up front, this was dovetailed into the requirements of the cockpit crew, providing it all fitted in with the midship hands. We had a lot of fun planning it all, and Mr Heath went along with virtually everything we suggested. This was done at more breakfast meetings, this time at 10 Downing Street or Chequers, the Prime Minister's official country home. There was a harmony among us all from the word go; we were excited and, from the first, felt that we were helping to organise a winner.

We knew, of course, that some pretty hot competition was being prepared in other camps, so selection for the team was by no means a foregone conclusion. We should have to prove by racing our brainchild that we had not only got a good hull and efficient layout, but that we could turn in the results. All this kept us keyed up to a high pitch as 1970 passed by. The boat was due to be laid down in October, and Olin and Rod Stephens were marvellous in the way they took our suggestions and turned them into working

Fig 13. Deck plan of
*Morning Cloud 2* by
courtesy of Sparkman
& Stephens Inc. This
was evolved after much
thought by the crew and
in close consultation
with the designers.

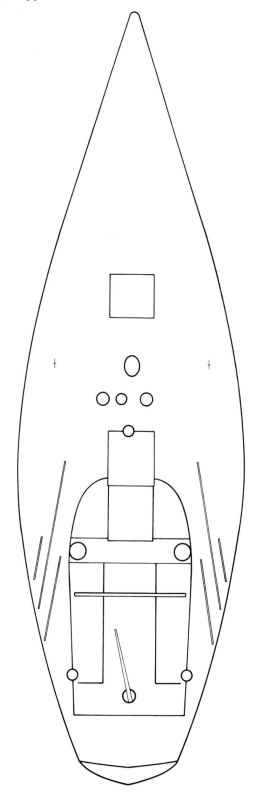

plans; sometimes, of course, they had to tell us that we could not have what we were asking, but they always came up with a good alternative. For instance, Anthony Churchill obviously had his ideas on how he wanted the navigation area laid out. These were put to the designers, who said whether it could be done or made suggestions for minor changes. Everything went forward happily and without a hitch, so that Lallows had the plans in plenty of time to start work at the beginning of the winter. And I was able to cross over to Cowes at any time to help iron out snags, but there were remarkably few.

The final layout of the boat was fairly radical by the standards of the day. We had taken the winches off the mast and mounted them on deck. It sounds ridiculous now to have to go on your knees to wind a winch, without benefit of a well cockpit, but this was all to reduce windage on the mast. The spinnaker pole lifts and down-hauls were all led aft to the cockpit. Our hatches were sliding, rather than up-and-over, to make it easier to pass sails through them (though we never really managed to make them water tight), and we had a seastay with a (single) luff groove for the genoa. We had a trim tab on the keel, copied from the twelves and not penalised by the rule in those days, and steering was by tiller.

Launching was in the spring of 1971, and from the first it was obvious that the boat was a flyer. She was what I call a forgiving boat, always ready to make amends for mistakes on the part of the crew. If you got a bad start it was almost as if she were saying 'So you made a mess of it. All right, I'll get you out of it.' And away she'd go, working her way to windward, passing other boats through their lee if necessary, until she got a clean wind.

**Selection**

We won practically everything we tried our hands at, so it was evident early on that we would be in the team. Another boat to do well was Arthur Slater's new *Prospect of Whitby*, who came good fairly soon after they had added some weight to her keel; Ian Lallow was sailing in her, as was my old mate from the *Kurrewa* days, Wally Smythers. The third boat was not so easy to choose, for there was a wealth of talent competing for the honour, among them a new *Noryema* for Ron Amey (his boat's name in his own name reversed, like Bill Citron's Dragon *Nortic*), Donald Parr's *Quailo* which was one of the new Nicholson 55's, and finally *Cervantes IV*, another Sparkman & Stephens design of about our size. The third place boiled down to a fight between these last two in the end, and finally Bob Watson's *Cervantes* got the nod.

Then, to cap our pleasure at being selected, the RORC announ-ced that Mr Heath was to be team captain. He, of course, was as delighted as we were, and entered into his duties with gusto. Being the man he is, he can quickly weld a team together–he had proved that to us in Australia, was doing it as Prime Minister, and now soon had everybody in the three British boats determined to win

Fig 14. Boisterous
weather did not stop us
hoisting the genoa as
well. The second *Cloud*
during one of the
Admiral's Cup races in
Cowes Week 1971.
*Photo: Beken*

honours for their country. The competition was very hot, and some really lovely boats were to be seen sailing in UK waters, as the fleet gathered together and indulged in the early warm-up races. *Morning Cloud* was a yacht to be really proud of. She was also the one they all wanted to see. Moored opposite the Groves and Gutteridge marina at Cowes, we were continually being asked if we would show people over her, and it made you feel good to know that it was our boat which everybody thought was the best laid out and equipped–and she was never more 'ours' than at those moments. We had put a lot of effort and time into perfecting her, and we might have been forgiven if we allowed our pride in her pre-eminent position to show. There was not another yacht to touch her, and the Japanese, who were just then entering serious racing for the first time, were particularly attentive with their cameras and gesticulations.

Mr Heath's translation to the top office in the land caused quite a stir in sailing circles, as you may imagine. The crew of *Morning Cloud* liked to think (quite incorrectly, I am sure) that they had helped in a small way to put him into 10 Downing Street. By winning the Sydney–Hobart race he had shown himself to be not only an able politician and statesman, but also a hard racing skipper, able to take all that the elements offered and come out on top of an international field; his personality blossomed to a new dimension in the light of the nationwide acclaim which he received.

But it also brought its problems. The security people started fussing around, and made all sorts of impractical suggestions; then the political pundits had to have their say regarding access, should the Skipper be needed on the helm at Westminster while he was steering his boat in an offshore race. We had to find room for a lot of heavy radio gear, and arrangements were proposed for lifting him off by helicopter if need arose. We didn't like the turn the plans were taking.

'What happens to *Morning Cloud* while all this is going on, sir?' I asked, speaking for us all and fearing the worst.

'Oh, she'll have to heave-to and lower her sails until it's all over,' was the reply from the Whitehall spokesman.

'To hell with that.' I knew I was voicing the opinion of the crew, but was equally aware that Mr Heath was also listening. 'We race to win and we don't stop for anybody, Prime Minister or no Prime Minister. If you want him, we'll put him over the side in a rubber dinghy and you can come and fetch him.'

'Excellent, excellent,' laughed Mr Heath, to my considerable relief as he turned to his advisors. 'That's the spirit I like to hear. You see gentlemen, you have your answer.'

## The Series

And so it was arranged. Fortunately we never had to do it, so I was not called upon to cast a Prime Minister adrift on the open sea. He

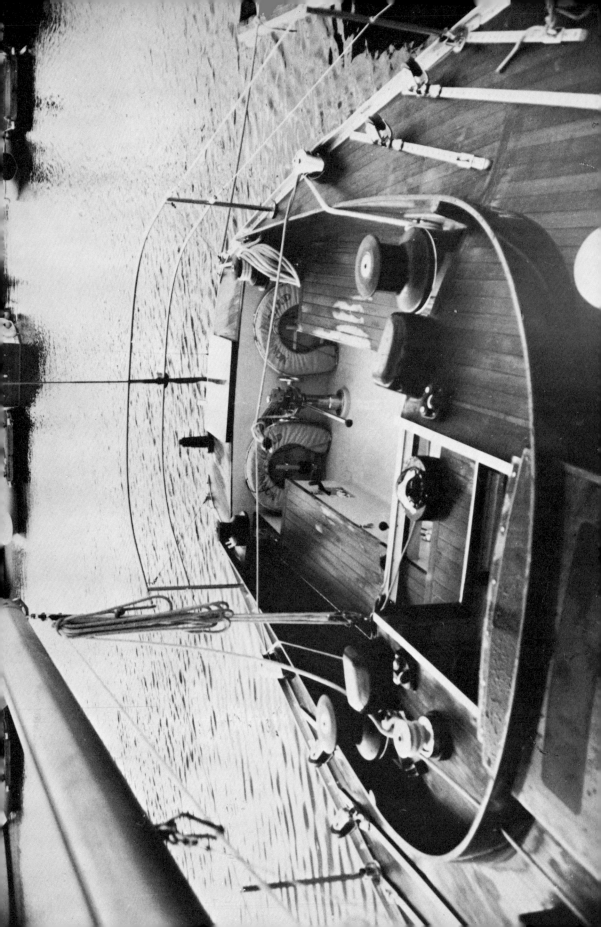

Fig 15. The simple
cockpit layout of
*Morning Cloud 2*, before
she was altered to a
wheel. There are two
spinnaker winches aft,
two linked genoa sheet
winches forward, and the
mainsheet winch to
starboard of the main
hatch. *Photo: Lewmar*

arranged his programme very well, and there were not a lot of races he had to miss. He planned to sail all the Admiral's Cup races, including the Fastnet and, though we seemed to be somewhat below our previous high standard, we did well enough to win the trophy. The team had a good Channel race, because *Prospect* won, we were third and *Cervantes* fourth, so we were off to a good points start. The first inshore race was a disappointment, for *Cervantes* was disqualified, but *Prospect* was second and we were fourth. This was a race which Mr Heath had to miss because he was kept in the House of Commons at the last minute. The Americans and Australians were now hard on our heels.

The *Cloud* then had a poorish tenth in the second inshore race, when we never seemed to get it together, and the Australians moved even closer. We had had a wonderful build-up, but then were unwise enough to take a month's lay off because we feared that we might become stale. As it happened, we went off the boil and never got back to our original form, so the actual racing was a bit of a let down. We have never let this happen in subsequent *Morning Clouds*. I think we unconsciously felt that the boat would lift us out of trouble as she had done before, but we were in a hot league now and couldn't afford any lapses. Then in the high scoring Fastnet race we carried away the track for the spinnaker pole on the fore side of the mast, which meant lashing the pole to the mast, with attendant problems every time we had to gybe. I don't offer this as an excuse, but we didn't do too well–it's funny, but none of the *Clouds* has ever had a good Fastnet. We didn't let the team down, because although Syd Fischer's *Ragamuffin* won that particular race for Australia, their team's chances were ruined when *Koomooloo* carried away her rudder. *Cervantes* made up for her earlier disqualification by coming third overall, and *Prospect* had a fairly good result.

It was enough to win the Admiral's Cup for Britain. We were all particularly pleased, because the Skipper was Prime Minister, and it can't have been easy for him to organise his time so that he could play a full part as team captain. In the middle of the series racing we had also collected the Gold Roman Bowl as overall winner of the Round the Island race for the third successive year–a feat never before or since achieved by one owner. The feeling of success and resulting jubilation remain with me to this day as one of the high spots of my career.

If the second *Cloud* had one failing, it was that she would never get above $8\frac{1}{2}$ knots down wind. Other boats would surf down a wave at a speed well above their theoretical maximum, but not us. We tried everything, from altering the rake to shifting weight; we even had crew members running forward as we dipped into a trough on the back of a wave and then doubling aft as we reached the bottom. I came to the conclusion that we would never do it, probably through some quirk of hull shape and immersed volume.

Although it was a broach which carried away our spinnaker pole tracks on the Fastnet, the boat did not display the unpleasant down wind habits of some fin and skeg designs, and she was pretty well mannered on the whole. We did have enough hard work on the tiller coming back from the Rock, with a 40 knot wind behind us, however, to make us decide to change to wheel steering for the 1972 season.

Above all, we were a happy ship. Mr Heath made an easy going skipper who could tolerate the odd mistake without undue displeasure, but woe betide the habitual offender! I have a pretty even temper myself, and got along with the Skipper very well. I recall one occasion, however, when he became rather repetitive about some point, so that I felt that we had heard enough.

'You are going on a bit,' I ventured. 'You're not in the House of Commons now, you know.'

We fed well on offshore races in all the *Clouds*. When the Skipper became Prime Minister, he had food specially prepared at Chequers and sent down, each dish labelled: Meal 1, Meal 2 and so on. The first race like this produced roast duckling with orange sauce, and fillet steaks with all the trimmings, so that we fed like lords–better I suspect, for I'd wager that the House of Lords Yacht Club never fared so well. We were then told to put it to the vote, and decided against this rather rich fare and asked whether we could have casseroles, stews, steaks (one of the easiest meals both to cook and to eat when you are standing on your ear), with plenty of soups. Similarly, we had been asked in the first *Morning Cloud* whether we wanted cans of beer on board, but we had voted for a 'dry' ship, going for colas, squash and the odd shandy which is always thirst quenching; I believe that there was half a bottle of medicinal brandy on board, but we never had cause to open it.

The crew took it in turns to heat the meals, but I must confess that I often found something else to do when it came to cooking anything other than a pot of tea; perhaps the shades of my early encounter with the paraffin stove on *Clover* were still haunting me. Then there has always been a hard tack box, with biscuits, chocolate wafers and boiled sweets for the night watch, or anyone else who was hungry between meals. We sail hard, we eat well and we leave the celebrating until we get ashore when, as I have already said, we go round together as a crew, skipper included.

# seven Evolution of the Morning Clouds

You will no doubt have noticed that evolution of design, materials and equipment has played a big part in improving speeds and reliability over the last two decades, and that I have been very much aware of this; my job and hobby have combined to put me in a position of considerable advantage in this respect, so I could hardly miss it. It may be of interest to trace the development of the various *Morning Clouds* with which I have been associated (and this is all of them so far), so that some of the thinking which goes on behind the scenes may be revealed. Tabulated below are the successive boats which Mr Heath has owned since he entered the offshore scene as an owner, together with some of their principal characteristics. The owner never numbers his boats but, for ease of reference, I have given each one a serial.

| Serial | Date | Designer | LOA | Berths | Crew | Remarks |
|---|---|---|---|---|---|---|
| 1 | 1969 | Sparkman & Stephens | 34' | 6 | 6 | Production fibreglass. 1st in Sydney–Hobart. |
| 2 | 1971 | ,, | 40' | 6 | 8 | Wood. AC team. |
| 3 | 1973 | ,, | 43' | 6 | 10 | Wood. Heavy disp. AC team. Lost at sea. |
| 4 | 1975 | ,, | 44' | 6 | 10 | Alloy |
| 5 | 1977 | Ron Holland | 44' | 8 | 10 | Alloy |

**Morning Cloud 1**

We have already seen that the first of the boats to bear the name *Morning Cloud* was a standard production boat, built in fibreglass, and which carried us to victory in the gruelling Sydney–Hobart race in December 1969. She was a good sea boat and, when we had played about with some minor points, was able to carry extra sail area to improve her performance in the less weighty winds of the southern hemisphere. Being a standard boat, her interior finish was good with a high degree of comfort. We each had our own berth, there was a good sized saloon table (which we used to put

Fig 16. The first *Morning Cloud*, a production S&S 34, racing in the Solent. *Photo: Beken*

ashore for racing), and the galley was equipped with one eye on the cruising man (and, because there was stowage, we in turn had a very full inventory of plates, pans and dishes). Sails were banished to the fo'cs'le or cockpit lockers, and there was usually a surprising air of space down below. She was the only *Cloud* with this comfort, and subsequent boats have become progressively more spartan inside.

It is interesting to note that *Morning After*, the first *Cloud's* sister ship, introduced us to the advantages of proper weight distribution. In a jump of a sea, they would sail to windward with the crew weight on the weather side, but down below. Keeping the weight low seemed to help, and was one more step in our progress to a full appreciation of the importance of keeping the ends of the boat light. When I think how in the *Sunmaids* we would all gather right aft in the cockpit, with the sails stowed out of the way as far forward as possible, I realise how much extra speed was there for the taking if only we had known. But then, look at almost any photograph of a boat taken in the 1950's and you will see a twisted mainsail; at least we had learned about kicking straps.

## Morning Cloud 2

The second boat, the one which was a flyer from the word go, sacrificed some of this luxury for better efficiency. We also spent a lot of time deciding deck layout, as I have said, but we left virtually the whole of the interior design to the Stephens brothers, apart from Anthony Churchill's navigation area. We still had six bunks but, as the crew had now increased to eight, it will be seen that there were not enough for everybody. The owner and the navigator, both of whom are liable on any racing boat to be called at any time (and so don't usually stand fixed watches), each had his own bunk–the two quarter berths in this case. These were, in fact, well forward, and the navigator's chart table was arranged so that the head of his bunk formed his seat when at work, an excellent arrangement from the navigator's point of view because, if he is not asleep, he can lay claim to the berth by sitting at his calculations. The rest of us chopped and changed in the remaining four, using the skipper's or navigator's if it was to windward and liable to be empty for a while. We tried to see that Mr Heath and Anthony had their own bunks when they needed them but, if the berth happened to be to leeward and we needed weight to windward, they dossed down where they could. We still had a saloon table but it was kept permanently ashore, and the light sails were still kept forward, but the whole layout was much less luxurious than the previous boat as we began to subordinate comfort to operational efficiency. We went to Hoods of Lymington for most of our sails and, like the previous boat, only had hydraulics on the backstay–but this was a terrific improvement on adjustment by rigging screw, which is normally too much trouble to touch except at the marina.

Fig. 17. The second *Morning Cloud* reaching beautifully; note the absence of turbulent water round the hull. I am sheet trimming by the mast. Peter Holt, who had sailed with me in *Sunmaid* and was a regular in this *Cloud*, seems to be reporting to Anthony Churchill, Sammy Sampson, Duncan Kay (ready on the spinnaker winch handle) and the Skipper. That's *Yeoman* ahead. *Photo: Beken*

This was the boat to which we all gave so much thought, and where the crew virtually designed the deck layout. Because Mr Heath was so good at listening to our ideas and then selecting those which he thought were good ones, we ended up with a highly efficient machine. It sounds unromantic to call a boat a machine, but that is what we were working towards, as we started to look on our boat much as a motor racing team must look on a Grand Prix car. Everything is relative, however, because that layout would be considered old fashioned in these days of multi-hydraulics, winches mounted round special crew wells, and bendy masts. *Morning Cloud 2* was a flyer all right and a forgiving boat, but she took a certain amount of working (I was younger in those days, and didn't mind winch grinding on my knees so much as I would now).

## Morning Cloud 3

In 1973 Mr Heath had a new boat; the Stephens brothers were once again the designers, and she was another wooden boat built at Lallows in Cowes. She was not the flyer that the previous boat had been and you may wonder why we had changed at all. Well, the rule had changed for one thing, and for another I rather think that Mr Heath wanted to do well in the Fastnet, which is generally reckoned to be a big boat's race and usually offers some strong winds.

Anyway, the third *Cloud* was bigger than the previous one, a good deal heavier, and was another step towards the completely functional boat. She had a tucked-in stern to take advantage of the rule, and once again we all had our say in the deck layout. This time we had a long trench running aft from the main hatch, which had been taken further forward than before in order to keep weight out of the ends–a lesson we were slowly learning. This trench had the halyard winches on either side of the forward end, and it ran back to open out aft into the cockpit proper; of course the whole thing was self draining. The genoa and spinnaker winches were mounted on either side of this cockpit, and we had a coffee grinder type pedestal in the middle which was linked to both the genoa sheet winches. It was a magnificent layout and an improvement on the previous arrangement; if nothing else, we no longer had to go on our knees to wind up a sail. There was also the advantage that the watch coming on deck for a sail change at night could remain in the dry and relative safety of this big cockpit, while those already night adapted went forward on deck.

Being bigger than the previous craft, this boat needed another two crew members; we only had six bunks though, so things got a bit hectic at times, particularly when you realise that we kept most of the sails around the mast when they were not in use. Only the spinnakers and other light sails were allowed forward, so we had to lash the rest tightly if we wanted any sort of walkway through the accommodation. We also had the inevitable saloon table to help fill the crowded space below, but we never fitted it; they seem to be an

Fig 18. *Morning Cloud 3* with both genoa and staysail under her spinnaker in the Solent in 1973. Ian Lallow is on the wheel. *Photo: Beken*

unavoidable part of the equipment and we must have a stack of them somewhere.

Anyway, this rather heavy boat was fast in any wind above 18 knots, but she was little short of painful in light weather. There is usually a dull spot in any offshore race, and the places we lost because the wind dropped on us were many, so we had to fight for our place in the Admiral's Cup team. We were lucky, in that we had some decent breezes for many of the selection races, so we put up quite a good showing–until the last one, that is, which was a disaster. We were leading as we rounded the CH 1 buoy just off the French coast and then the wind fell away as we were coming back across the English Channel to the Nab Tower, so everyone–and I mean everyone–passed us. The selectors were kind, reckoning that we had generally sailed the boat pretty well and that this was a freak result, so we were included, but it was by no means a foregone conclusion. Mr Heath found that his duties as Prime Minister would not allow him to guarantee to be on every race, so Donald Parr of *Quailo* was named team captain. But we did not do too well, and the Germans carried all before them with ruthless efficiency and good sailing.

*Morning Cloud 3* was the one which suffered the terrible tragedy of losing two men on the passage from Ramsgate to the Solent. Approaching the Owers in force 10, they were unlucky enough to be caught by a freak wave, and the boat dropped off the top of it onto her side, losing two men overboard in the process. Unfortunately one of their harness lines broke and, in returning to look for Nigel Cummings who was in the water, they were struck by another rogue sea which washed overboard Mr Heath's godson, Christopher Chadd, as he was in the main hatch just making his way on deck. This time the boat, heavy weather sea boat though she was, and beautifully built by one of the best yards in the country, started to break up near one of the hatches as she crashed into the trough. To cut a long story short, Nigel and Christopher were not recovered and the survivors had to take to the life raft; they were eventually washed ashore in an exhausted condition.

As I have already mentioned, the third *Cloud* did us well, for we made the British team for the defence of the Admiral's Cup in 1973. We had not got into the team so easily as last time, but some good results in medium to heavy weather helped, as did the presence of Ian Lallow, son of the Cowes boatbuilder and a first rate inshore helmsman who knows the Solent well. We had a full suit of Hood sails, with one or two Banks starcut reachers. Once again we had an indifferent Fastnet race, and we lost the Admiral's Cup to the well prepared Germans. They, like the Americans, had quickly learned the importance of proper draft control in sails, and this helped them to sweep the board. But the fact that the British usually bounce back again shows that we learn things too, though not perhaps quite so fast.

Just prior to the loss of his boat, Mr Heath had decided that the

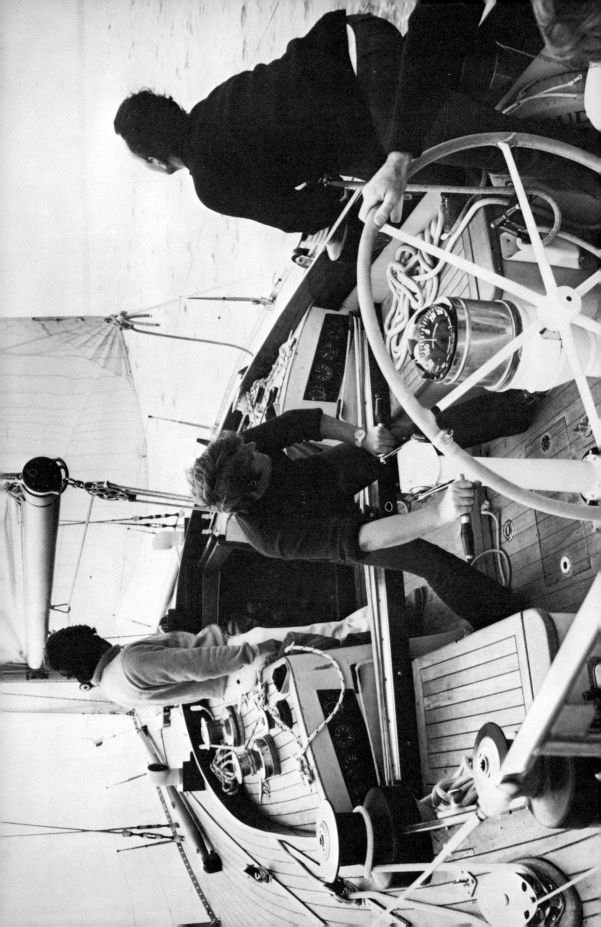

Fig 19. *Morning Cloud 3* had full linkage from the pedestal to the sheet winches. This picture shows the ease of operation and co-ordination between winchman and sheet trimmer.
*Photo: Anthony Linton, courtesy Lewmar*

financial state of the country was too uncertain for him to indulge in a new design for 1975. Number three had always been as stiff as a church–in fact she was known by some of the boys as 'the church'– and we had been going to lengthen her mast by three or four feet and take some of the weight off her keel in an attempt to give her a better light weather performance. That was not to be, however, and the insurance money was put into a new boat.

## Morning Cloud 4

When Mr Heath could turn his mind to the question of replacement after the tragedy, we started discussing who should design her. The crew felt that the time had come to change from Sparkman & Stephens, and to try one of the up and coming younger men; we had three different people in mind. As we were far from unanimous, the Skipper decided not to leave the firm he knew and who had done us so well in the past. So Olin and Rod drew us another set of lines about the same size as the one we had just lost, but with the idea that she would be better in light weather.

For the first time we would be having an alloy boat in an attempt to keep the displacement down, and the hull was built by Allday Aluminium and finished off by Camper & Nicholson at Gosport. Mr Heath was, I think, tempted once or twice to build abroad but, apart from a natural wish to place the work in Britain, he liked to be able to visit his boats at frequent intervals while they were building. He would go down to inspect progress and discuss any problems which the builders had encountered; in addition he liked to have a photographic record of all stages of construction. He was thus in an excellent position to conduct the regular crew meetings he used to convene in order to pool ideas and views–think tanks, I suppose you could call them.

The message about keeping weight out of the ends of the boat had really got home now, and all the six bunks were in the middle third of the hull. Once again there were two quarter berths for the owner and the navigator. We then had four immediately forward of these, one over the other on each side of the central area–I won't call it a saloon, because there was no table (except perhaps in the store?), the genoas were stowed three aside under the lower of the two-tiered bunks, and the galley was somewhat bare, to put it mildly. We spent a certain amount of time designing the bunks so that we should need no leeboards. Basically we had a canvas hammock, with an alloy rail each side, slung deep enough for there to be no risk of falling out, yet you could roll out easily when required, without the hassle of untying or unshipping leeboards. A thin mattress was taken right over the top of the rail each side, so that it did not cut into your back.

We had twin forehatches to go with our twin headsail luff grooves. The idea was that one sail could be lowered down one hatch while the replacement was being pulled up through the other and straight onto the grooved stay. There were hydraulics on

the backstay, babystay and kicking strap, so that we had good control over mast bend. We stowed virtually nothing in the overhangs, and only the spinnakers were kept forward of the main bulkhead. The theory of keeping weight in the middle of the boat is all very well, but it doesn't help very much if the hull hasn't got what it takes. I don't like to blame a boat for poor performance, but every design team produces the odd failure, I don't care who they are. Unfortunately this was one of the rare S & S disappointments and, try as we might, we could not get her to go. She was super when reaching and running, but she did not have the usual S & S windward ability in a seaway, when she tended to 'hobbyhorse'. Funnily enough, she was quite a good boat offshore, when she was able to sail over the rather longer waves, particularly when we kept the weight out of the stern–unlike a lot of Stephens designs, which seem to like to have the rudder well down in the water.

I have always maintained that a 75 per cent winning boat sailed by a 100 per cent winning crew will succeed, whereas a 100 per cent winning boat sailed by a 75 per cent winning crew will not, but I fear that *Morning Cloud 4* was rather less than the required 75 per cent.

Olin Stephens came with us on the 1975 Round the Island Race (readers with retentive memories will recall that we had recently won it three years in a row), and we did quite well for two thirds of the 65 mile distance. Then the wind went light and came ahead, so that we virtually stopped.

'I see what you mean,' said Olin as the rest of the fleet sailed past and drew away.

Part of the trouble lay in excessive flare at the bows, which caused the sea to knock her off too much, but she just had not got that touch of Stephens genius which we had come to expect.

Anthony Churchill decided to race the 1975 season in *More Opposition*, owned by Tony Morgan who was a business associate of his, and we missed him dearly because he had been part of the team since the word go–longer than I had. But we were lucky enough to get the services of Peter Nicholson as navigator and relief helmsman. Apart from anything else, as his firm had built the boat he had a vested interest in seeing that she did well. We had an excellent wardrobe of Hood sails, and the deck layout was an improvement on the past. Nevertheless we failed to get into the Admiral's Cup team (was this a pointer to the importance of keeping a winning combination together?) from a strong field of contenders, so we started thinking again in terms of a new designer for 1977, and the general opinion among the crew was that Ron Holland, the young New Zealander, would do a good job. Mr Heath felt the same way as well, so he decided to approach him.

## Morning Cloud 5

Ron Holland's *Cloud* was conceived to take advantage of the latest changes in the IOR. As the committee did not meet until

November, the designer had to wait until then before he knew what the final rules would be. This meant a rather rushed job, and the boat was not lofted until after Christmas; she was launched and ready for trials in April–a rather late start in life.

She was very fine forward and floated bow down without the crew aboard (which gave an advantage when measuring for the rating); as she only floated to her marks when the crew was aboard and aft, all the bunks were in the aft third of the hull. In addition all the sails had to be aft and, because we now had eight bunks, there was not much room to move when they were all taken out of their bins and brought aft for racing. Not to put too fine a point on it, this was a bloody nuisance because there seemed to be sailbags wherever you went. They were in the way if you wanted to go to the heads, if you wanted to reach the galley, or if you wanted to get into your bunk; everyone except the navigator had to crawl over sails to get anywhere. All Admiral's Cup boats seem to have this problem these days, and sorting out the right sail can be tricky. We try to guess what canvas we are most likely to need for the early stages of a race, and then stow the sailbags where the right ones come most easily to hand.

This was the lightest *Cloud* to date, and disposal of crew weight was most important, particularly in view of her fine forward end, which caused her to bury her nose as soon as there was any weight forward of the mast. In all but very light winds the watch below always slept to windward, while those on deck were, indeed, on the deck up to windward and not in the cockpits; this was especially important on a shy spinnaker reach. You will notice that I used the plural when talking about the cockpits; we had two, one for the helmsman, the navigator and the mainsheet man, and one for the genoa sheet trimmers and the midship men. While there are certain advantages in this, there is more to be gained from one large cockpit, where crewmen can switch roles rapidly.

In addition to the three hydraulic controls which we had had on the previous boat, we now had hydraulic adjustment of the forestay, so sail shape and thrust were variable to say the least; but the rule soon had something to say about all this movement of the mast. It is worth commenting at this point that shifting the masthead can alter weather helm so dramatically that there is a danger of being caught out with too much canvas. As the wind gets up, the helmsman finds that he can control the boat with such a light touch if everything is set right (forward rake reduces weather helm), that he fails to notice that the boat is leaning on her ear, and would thus go faster if she were not pressed so hard. The lesson is to watch the angle of heel, which will tell you the true story.

There are so many variables on board these days that the correct setting for any given circumstances demands a meticulous record of the combination. You have to check the right headsail with the right fairlead, the mainsheet traveller position, mast rake and bend (involving forestay, backstay, babystay and kicking strap hydraulic pressures at the correct settings, and the running

Fig 22. *Morning Cloud 5*
deck layout, showing the
characteristic Holland
stern of 1977. The
flattening reef is down
and the genoa has been
barberhauled to a second
block on the rail.
*Photo: Beken*

backstays set up properly), flattening reef and cunningham hole, clew outhaul and leechlines; you also have to watch the angle of heel as well as fore and aft trim. Then as like as not the helmsman will complain.

'I've got too much weather helm. Give me a bit more on the babystay, please.' But he might not say 'please'.

So the whole rigmarole has to be gone through again, while the navigator watches the closehauled indicator and the water speed, rather like an airline pilot running through his take-off check list: babystay, backstay, runners, traveller . . .

Five weeks is not enough time to tune a new boat unless you work hard at it and keep very full notes.

## A Spell Ashore

At the beginning of 1977 I had a bit of trouble with my health, and Mr Heath made me see his doctor in London to get a second opinion after my own had looked me over. He was always very good like that. I remember one day back in the early seventies when a spinnaker sheet winch pulled off the second *Morning Cloud* and pinned my wrist against a block in the pulpit, so that I thought I was going to lose my arm; the winch itself whistled past, cracking me on the knee. Mr Heath was Prime Minister at the time and had to get back to London immediately after the accident, but first he had his chauffeur take me to hospital in his car, and found time to ring up from Downing Street to ask how I was. I had to go on crutches for a while and the doctor advised against going on the Fastnet. As George Stead, one of our stalwarts at the time, had had to cry off already, I realised that it would be next to impossible to find another replacement at such short notice. I was glad of an excuse to put aside my crutches, and after a day or two of scrambling round a boat on the open water my leg gave me no more trouble.

Anyway, to get back to 1977, I was told that I had to give up sailing or my job for three or four months. I was still busily engaged in the affairs of Montague Smith and felt that there was no way I could take this sort of time off from the office–in any case, the firm had been marvellous to me over the years, and it would have been most unfair to have deserted them like that for the entire summer. So I told the Skipper that I would help tune the new boat after she was launched at the beginning of the 1977 season, but that I would not be available to race. It was decided that Peter Nicholson would take over as tactician and also be in charge of the day to day running of the boat; Anthony Churchill came back as navigator and Iain MacDonald-Smith came into the crew from North Sails instead of Pete Dove (we had switched to North for our sails on this boat, so this was a logical move). Peter Nicholson brought one or two of his own crew with him, so there was a fairly new team.

I must say that, after over twenty years of hard sailing every summer, I was ready for a break. Don't forget that, besides the actual sailing, I had had to give quite a lot of time to the boat and to the crew, so it meant that a lot of work had to be fitted into the office routine somehow. I did not even go to Cowes Week that year, and was glad to be free of all responsibilities. Naturally, I followed *Morning Cloud*'s progress, and was nearly as disappointed as they must have been when they were just pipped for third place in the Admiral's Cup team by Robin Aisher's *Yeoman XX* (the same Peterson design which had led the successful British attempt to wrest the trophy back from the Germans two years previously); selection hung in the balance until the last two short races, when neither boat did brilliantly, but Robin got the better result. *Morning Cloud* was nominated as reserve–an honour which carries little responsibility or opportunity, but serves perhaps to soften the blow a little. It had been useful for the Southern Cross series in 1969, because it had meant that we got the benefit of the cheap air fares offered by Qantas and were in on all the social functions and team planning in Australia, so we did not feel left out on our own. The boat had had a rather short preparation, due to her late start in life, and the boys felt that they were just beginning to weld the crew together and get results. As it turned out, if they had been chosen for the team instead of *Yeoman*, Britain would not have retained the cup, as Chris Dunning (*Marionette*), Jeremy Rogers (*Moonshine*–a production boat which did extraordinarily well to finish second in the overall points standings) and Robin Aisher (*Yeoman XX*) succeeded in doing so well.

### Back in Harness

In September the old urge crept over me again, and I found myself wanting to get back afloat. I did the last Solent points races of the season with *Morning Cloud*, but she was not entered for Burnham Week that year and was laid up quite early on. I got the feeling that Mr Heath was a bit despondent and asked him whether he would be fitting out again in 1978.

'You don't suppose I would end my racing career on last year's results, do you?' he asked, with a flicker of the old enthusiasm.

### Sails

I cannot claim to have been personally involved in the develop-ment of sails since we tried setting a genoa with a spinnaker in the *Sunmaid* days, and then helped to perfect the twin pole spinnaker gybe evolved with Chippy Davy and John Oakeley. But *Morning Cloud* has always been ready to adapt to any improvement such as multi-hydraulics, jiffy reefing or better sailbags. I have mentioned the big boy once or twice, so perhaps a few words on this controversial sail might not come amiss.

There are fairly precise limits within which the sail has its uses,

Fig 23. Deck plan of *Morning Cloud 5*, by courtesy of Ron Holland Designs. This shows the development which has taken place over the years.

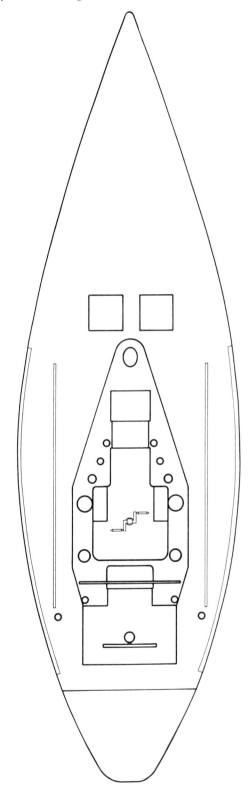

and these are worth defining because it certainly helps steady the boat in rolling conditions down wind. But it only pays when the wind is greater than about 8 knots and is within 30 degrees of dead aft; when you remember that a dead run is not a particularly efficient point of sailing (in the *Cloud* we always try to have the wind at least 10–15 degrees on the quarter when running), you are down to a relative wind angle of 10–30 degrees of the stern and a condition of force 3 or over.

The big boy, or blooper, seems to have a great attraction for the crew, probably because it is quickly set or handed and needs no complicated gear to get it going. With this in mind, many a foredeck gang will enthusiastically suggest it and as willingly spend time fiddling with halyard and sheet (but the helmsman will not usually be among those voting for it, because it renders him virtually blind ahead).

'If you ease the spinnaker pole a little, the big boy will draw better,' they cry.

So the danger is that the real big one will be neglected for the better trim of the lesser sail. Don't get me wrong, I'm all in favour of the blooper, providing it remains subordinate to the spinnaker and is not trimmed at the expense of the latter.

We should not have been taken by surprise quite so much when Chris Bouzaid first sprang the sail on us, because *Vendetta* had used her light genoa in exactly this way at Burnham in the sixties, and we had seen it many a time when racing against her. But, like many other ideas, it only caught on when used to good effect in good company. One man sets a particular sail and does well, so the rest follow him like a lot of sheep, even though it may be the way he is holding the tiller which is winning the race for him and not the canvas he sets. So we get the spinnaker staysail, tallboy, big boy and now the very specialist reacher. At one time if there was a gap which could be filled, you pushed canvas into it in order to trap the wind without worrying how it got away. Nowadays we usually carry a high cut reacher under the spinnaker, set flying with the tack three or four feet aft of the stem; sometimes we set both genoa and staysail with the spinnaker. In these days of restrictions on the number of sails which may be carried, we have a second tack eye fitted to the luff of the reacher roughly opposite the clew. In this way the sail can also provide a double head rig when close fetching under genoa at 40–45 degrees from the wind, but the reacher then has a shorter hoist to avoid spoiling the slot aloft.

Spinnakers which are too big are a damn nuisance. They flop about the foredeck in light winds, make the helmsman partially blind and can be a hell of a problem to trim. It is not a coincidence that the $\frac{7}{8}$ths rig is making a comeback. Hulls are more easily driven these days, and they surf more readily (certainly more so than our second boat which, as I have said, wouldn't get out of her own bed). This being so, what is the point of extra canvas when you are already off the clock? So smaller spinnakers are regaining their popularity–and thank God say I, and everybody else who has ever been forward of the mast in anger. The boat will broach less, is more stable and the helmsman (that man who is sometimes forgotten by the foredeck gang as they wrestle with acres of thrashing sail) can see more. I tell you, when the wind is over 15 knots, *Morning Cloud* uses a cutter rig when it is 60–70 degrees off, even 80, rather than the tri-radial; when it gets up to 30 knots, we will sometimes be seen with the same rig when the wind is 10 degrees aft of the beam. But then we're special–I'm a renegade foredeck gorilla, now basking in the warmth of the afterguard position, so I can give the orders; but the spinnaker hands know damn well that I've been there, and can still do everything they can do just as quick. So it's a bold man who queries my decisions.

## Crew

We reckon these days to have two helmsmen of international standard as regular crew members. In this way we can be sure of having one on deck at most times, and there will usually be at least one other good helmsman in the watch who can alternate with him as required, and be under his eye, so to speak. All these helmsmen are experienced racing men who can double at most jobs round the boat. The arrival of bending masts and intricate control of sail shape and centre of effort has caused us to look at the dinghy classes for helmsmen, because it is there that draft control has been studied carefully over the years. Ocean racers are being sailed like open boats these days, and the sensitive touch and fine control necessary have been part of the way of life of dinghy sailers for a long time.

# eight People and Places

Of all the nationalities I have raced with and against, I would have to list four at the top: in alphabetical order, Americans, Australians, Germans and New Zealanders.

## New Zealanders

You might be surprised to see the last of these in my personal league table, but I'm not sure but what they don't come out on top. I first came across them in 1968 at Heligoland, when I was sailing in *Morningtown* with Mike Winfield in the One-Ton Cup series. The Germans retained the trophy with *Optimist*, but Chris Bouzaid came a very good second in *Rainbow*, no mean feat having travelled half way round the world to race in strange surroundings (he won it the next year).

Whereas we liked to think that we sailed pretty well and had a good boat in *Morningtown*, Chris and his boys really worked at it. They went for a run before breakfast every day, did physical exercises and sailed in wet-suits, of all things. We couldn't understand it–until we saw them race. They got under way well over an hour before everyone else each time, and went out to sail up and down the line, then they practised starts at each end and in the middle, taking bearings as they did so. On the race they strapped that boat down and fairly belted her along.

I remember one race when *Morningtown* was ahead of *Rainbow* and there was 25–30 knots of wind right up our tails. Suddenly the New Zealanders started to go by us, and we saw that they had three men on the bow as they dipped into the swell which was running– and it can be big out there in the North Sea. On the way down the trough these three chaps ran aft to change the trim of the boat and keep her on the plane, and she absolutely surged past us to the accompaniment of her crew's excited cheers. All this time we were sitting in our cockpit trimming the spinnaker nicely and 'yacht-ing'; Chris Bouzaid's boys were 'yacht racing', and they kept it up for three hours all the way to the finishing line. Most un-British and they taught us a lesson.

When I was commenting on this afterwards, one of the other British crewmen present told me that he had been aboard a Camper & Nicholson 50-footer in the 1967 Sydney–Hobart. One

night it was blowing about force 8, so that they were under storm
canvas flying a tiny spitfire jib, when suddenly they heard a terrific
clatter and rattle astern of them, and out of the gloom came Chris
Bouzaid in *Rainbow* with a spinnaker up, if you can believe it. She
roared past in a flurry of spray with everything moaning and
groaning, and shot into the night. Mark you, there is not quite the
weight of wind in the warm northerlies down there, but this was
win or bust, and they won. Yes, they are a tough crowd.

In 1971 the second *Morning Cloud* was chosen with *Prospect of
Whitby III* and *Cervantes IV* to represent Britain in the Southern
Cross series, so this time we were going as a full member of the
team. Mr Heath couldn't come with us, so Sammy Sampson was
put in charge of the boat and George Stead came into the crew as
replacement helmsman; team captain was Arthur Slater in
*Prospect*. We knew that, apart from the American and various
Australian State entries, Chris Bouzaid would be leading a team of
New Zealand One-Tonners.

We reckoned that we were a pretty formidable combination and,
indeed, we were. In the *Cloud*, of course, we had the added
incentive of trying to get our name on the winners board of the
Sydney–Hobart for the second time running. Perhaps we all
allowed our self-confidence to grow too strong, at all events we did
not ask so many questions about conditions as we had two years
previously, and we paid dearly for it–twice.

First, we were racing out of Sydney on the medium race and had
to go round a mark to the south, then past Bird Island to the north
before a final 60 odd miles beat home. On rounding Bird Island we
calculated in *Morning Cloud* that we must be lying second on
corrected time. Syd Fischer in the big *Ragamuffin*, fresh from his
overall victory in the Fastnet the previous August, was in sight
ahead, and he tacked out to sea; just ahead of us *Cervantes* tacked
inshore and so did most of the others following behind. But we
were happy that the captain of the Australian team must know the
local conditions, so away we went after *Ragamuffin*. In the event,
the wind freed on the inshore tack so that they all got a lift along
the shore and laid the mark; it headed us on the other tack out to
sea and, when we came about, we found that we had overstood so
had to ease sheets. The inshore fleet all romped home ahead of us
and *Cervantes* won the race. Meanwhile the wind promptly headed
us again, and we had to put in another tack to lay the mark. We
should, of course, have covered the boats astern of us and not
bothered about *Ragamuffin*, who was a good deal bigger than us
and was bound to beat us in anyway.

The second tactical error came during one of the short inshore
races. We were sailing just that little bit more free than the rest of
the opposition, because we thought that the next mark lay further
to leeward than they all seemed to consider, because they were all
holding up to windward. Our navigator checked and re-checked,
then somebody spotted the mark nicely ahead of us. Up went the
star-cut spinnaker and we romped along, glad to have our

calculations confirmed and happily watching the rest of them clawing too far to windward.

But we hadn't reckoned with the dreaded set, which we had used to such good effect in 1969. This time it only came in evidence when we were about a mile from the buoy, and we discovered why the rest were up to windward–we were being carried sideways at about two knots. In the end even coming hard on the wind was not enough, and we had to put in a short tack, to find the rest of the fleet thundering down on the other board with eased sheets. Having been brought up among the tides of the Solent, I of all people should have known never to throw away the weather

Fig 24. The second *Morning Cloud* and *American Eagle* in very light weather just after the start of the 1971 Sydney–Hobart. The converted 12-metre was first to finish and we were fourth on corrected time.
*Photo: Australian Information Service*

gauge, particularly when the opposition were practically shouting at us. The fact that we were revelling in sailing without having to worry about tidal streams should not have lulled us into a false sense of security, and we should have been alert to suspicion.

In spite of all this, the team acquitted itself well, and came second for the second time running. The trophy was taken by the New Zealanders sailing their One-Tonners; these smaller boats are allowed in the Southern Cross series, and we found in 15 knots of wind that they were going as fast as we were. Their boats were two S&S designs and a Carter, all of fairly conventional lines, which they sailed in typically aggressive style. They romped the inshore races and were all well up in the Sydney–Hobart despite the fact that, with only 60 miles to go, we were up with *Ragamuffin* and *Prospect*, and a good 25 miles ahead of the smaller boats. Admittedly there was under 5 knots of wind, but you can't have everything and it was only a question of time before it filled in. It did, but from astern, for the evening radio position reports put the small New Zealand boats only five or six miles back, and they brought a 20 knot following wind with them. By nightfall it had reached force 8 or 9 and we couldn't even boom out the genoa. In one of the brief periods of relative quiet Sammy Sampson, who had been asleep in his bunk below and was possibly feeling his responsibilities as owner's representative, put his head out of the main hatch.

'Don't you think we'd be better with the spinnaker?' he asked.

At that moment we shipped a green wave straight into the cockpit.

'Sorry I spoke,' spluttered Sammy, now drenched to the skin, and disappeared below again. We didn't have to say a word.

*Morning Cloud* was first in her class, but we were only fourth overall, so our name was not to be repeated on the trophy board.

It was during this series that Chris Bouzaid produced the big boy on one of the inshore races. When we saw it flying to such good effect (or imagined good effect), a check on the rules seemed to show that it was illegal. Arthur Slater told us to go ahead with a protest against *Rainbow*, which we duly did in order to get a qualified deliberation and a ruling on the sail. As we all know, it was declared legal, partly because the sheet was led right outside the spinnaker sheet which was technically important, and so the protest was thrown out. Chris, being a sailmaker, had a sail which was specially shaped to suit the task, but the rest of the fleet soon found that their light genoas did a reasonable job and we all sprouted bloopers from then to the end of the series.

### Australians

Turning to the Australians, I have already written something of them in the chapter on the Sydney–Hobart. We had a wonderful opportunity to see some of the country between races, and we made the most of it. Syd Fischer owned a super hotel where he kindly gave us very good terms, and we enjoyed the novelty of a swimming pool on the seventeenth floor and a revolving restaurant, all in sight of the magnificent harbour with its futuristic opera house. The hospitality at Sydney was only equalled by that of the Tasmanians when we finally got there at the end of the race.

Being a hard sailing, tough nation, Australians have no time for the man who cannot take it. Englishmen have a reputation down under for soft living, which it takes a while to live down, but once you have shown that you can meet them on their own ground, with no quarter asked or given, they take you straight to their hearts which, though they might strongly deny it, are made of solid gold. You cease being a Pommie and become a Brit. The English manner of speech, of course, is a sure target for any Australians keen to take the mickey out of a Pom, and I have often been asked how they took to Mr Heath's almost exaggerated accent. I don't know what they said in private, but I do know that they found it impossible to understand how I, with my strong Hampshire burr, could come from the same country as the Skipper. But they quickly found that Mr Heath was a good mixer, as tough as they were when it came to competition (he was the first Brit to carry off their big one since John Illingworth won the inaugural race back in 1945), a man who asked no special favours, and was content to be judged on his merits. They particularly liked the way he was inseparable from his crew on all social occasions.

A brief comment should serve to illustrate Australian dedication. I recall one Cowes Week when an Aussie boat missed out a mark in one of the Admiral's Cup inshore races, right after the start. On being told of this as she came in, she turned right round and resailed the entire five hour course just to pick up the team points for coming in last.

## Germans

Having won the One-Ton Cup with *Optimist* at Le Havre in 1967, the Germans had, of course, been at Heligoland in strength to defend it the following year. As we know, their determination and thoroughness saw them through, and *Optimist* retained the trophy. They had begun their assault on the offshore scene. Their crews were husky young chaps with short hair cuts, and bristling with the efficiency well suited to this kind of cut and thrust racing.

Something more, however, is needed in the handicap fleet and they had to wait for the Admiral's Cup until 1973. That was the year we had the third *Morning Cloud* built and just scraped into the third slot in the British team, as is related elsewhere, but we failed to retain the trophy we had won in 1971. The Germans brought three new boats to the Solent, showed us that they had prepared themselves magnificently, and had also added that touch of flair which had been missing from their earlier more disciplined approach to racing. Their determined assault on the Cup proved to be irresistible, and they went home deservedly triumphant after the final race of the series to the Fastnet Rock and back. They are always a force to be reckoned with, particularly when they really want something.

## Americans

Next in this round-up of the principal sailing nationalities, we come to the Americans. Their reputation for drive and energy is not ill-founded and, when you add the fact that many of their top international sailors are wealthy men, you have a formidable combination. American industry benefits from the talents of many nations whose restless citizens have sought a better life in the New World. Their technology is advanced and they have the imagination to profit from it. So their gear is always first class; I don't think I have ever seen poor equipment on a top American ocean racer. And their crews usually have just the right combination of youth and experience to generate keenness and judgement. It may offend both nations if I liken them to the Australians, but there is a common background of self-reliance which breeds a certain assertive ability to drive a boat with skill and energy. Also, like the Australians, Americans are hospitable to a fault and can never do enough for a crew which may have come half way round the world to race with them.

## Other Countries

Of the other nations, the Latin countries seem to do well, with Italy and Brazil well to the fore, and Spain and France showing flashes of brilliance–France won the Fastnet with *Pen Duick III* in 1967 and Brazil did it with *Saga* in 1973, followed by *Sayula*'s wonderful performance round the world the next year. Nor must we forget the Dutch, who have a seafaring tradition which is not unlike our own.

I have already told of the high standard of efficiency and helmsmanship which the 34 ft S&S designed *Hestia* brought to the Solent in the 'sixties and caused us all to start looking for ways to improve boat speed. Peter Vroon certainly made his mark on Cowes Week in 1977 by winning 6 out of 7 races with *Formidable* the former *Marionette*, which he had bought from Chris Dunning; we managed to take one race off him, but he beat us by a minute or so every other time and, to cap it all, he had the ex-owner on board once or twice just to show him what a bargain he had got. And, of course, Cornelius van Rietschoten has shown what stamina the Dutch possess by winning the 1977/78 Whitbread Round the World Race in *Flyer*.

## Japanese

Finally we come to the latest nation to emerge on the international offshore scene: the Japanese. They have entered the game with the thoroughness which you would expect from such a hardy seafaring race. Profiting from the American influence, they have long built boats for the US market and thus have developed an industry along modern lines. Now their naval architects are working in American and British design offices, and they are swift to take up ideas from all over the world–the popular conception of the Japanese with his camera and flair for copying is no myth. After their victory in the Quarter-Ton Worlds in 1978, it may not be long before they frighten some people in the Admiral's Cup.

### British

We should not, I suppose, leave this summary without a brief self-analysis. The British have always been slow to change, and it has taken us some time to become as thorough and determined as some of our rivals. But we have at last learned the lesson and this is in no small measure due to the selection for the Admiral's Cup team of some of the younger men like Robin Aisher, Jeremy Rogers and Chris Dunning. Our gear is now as good as any in the world, our most recent teams could not have been better and it has been marvellous to watch their performance. We may be slow to learn, but we hoist in the message in the end.

Perhaps the point about my own countrymen which has been the most evident to one who has been on the inside, has been their wonderful esprit de corps. On board the various boats I have crewed in, we have usually generated a partisan feeling against all comers which has been in the best of spirits, yet this has quickly turned to one of co-operation and corporate involvement as soon as three boats are combined into a team. People from all walks of life have got on marvellously well together, and the only yardstick is not how you eat or speak, but whether you can do your job and not get other people's backs up.

### Sailing Grounds

Of all the waters I have sailed in, Sydney stands out most in my memory. For beautiful scenery, it takes a lot of beating. You can do a thirty mile race in the harbour and never be away from the most breathtaking shoreline. One moment you will be tacking right underneath overhanging trees so that you touch the branches, and the next, sailing along miles of sandy beaches; then you will be passing the magnificent Opera House or going under the vast expanse of the bridge to the inner harbour. Further delights await you outside, with place names to make the imagination run riot: Wollongong, Bulli and Botany Bay; while Newcastle, Swansea and Liverpool conjure up links with the Old Country. When I was first asked which was the most memorable venue I have ever sailed in, Sydney came unhesitatingly to my lips–partly perhaps because of the success we had from there in 1969. And then I remembered Newport, Rhode Island.

Fig 25. Sydney is one of
the finest sailing grounds
in the world. The Opera
House and the bridge
add to the splendour of
the natural scenery, and
you can enjoy a 30 mile
race within the harbour
itself.
*Photo: The Australian
Information Service,
London*

What a wonderful sailing ground! To the west is the somewhat humid expanse of Long Island Sound, nearly a hundred miles from east to west and leading to New York itself; to the east is Martha's Vineyard, Nantucket Island and round the corner to Cape Cod. What a wealth of cruising grounds is there, and no wonder there are thousands of Americans who are content to explore the countless bays and inlets with never a thought for racing.

I was lucky enough to sail in the Southern Ocean Racing Conference (SORC) series with David May's *Winsome* at the beginning of 1973. This takes place in and around Florida, and I saw more of any country during two short months than ever before. We started at St Petersburg, a fine old town 200 miles up the west coast of Florida in the Gulf of Mexico. It has a superb marina with every facility the yachtsman could wish, and which is in sharp contrast to the somewhat quiet nature of the town, a place where many Americans go to live out their retirement.

I do know that we had expected to find hot weather when we arrived, but were surprised to find it snowing when we got there, so we had to dash out and buy some warm clothing. Our first race was to Venice, a few miles to the South. What a gem of a place, with lots of palm trees–remembered also because of the interesting trip back to St Petersburg. We went through the inland waterways under engine the whole way, with a wonderful insight into the countryside.

The big race of the SORC, their equivalent to the Fastnet, if you like, is the 370 mile run round the southern tip of Florida and up to Fort Lauderdale. This is a great place and I preferred it to the somewhat brash nature of Miami with its big city problems. From Lauderdale we raced to Lucaya in the Grand Bahama, back to Miami for the Lipton Cup, then another longish one to Nassau before finally ending the series with the Nassau Cup.

The Bahamas would be all right if you had plenty of money. When we were there the islands were waiting impatiently for their independence, and things were a little unsettled, so perhaps I did not see them in the best light. We did a quick cruise in the area on our way back to Miami and were lucky enough to be offered hospitality at Cat's Cay, the American-owned resort where you can get nowhere without money and a lot of it. Everything is larger than life and exactly like something out of a Hollywood movie set. For the first time in my life I found myself envying the rich and the life they led, but I can't help wondering whether it wouldn't all get rather monotonous in the end.

The beaches at Nassau are superb, as they are in most of the islands. The water is clear, coral abounds and palm trees sway on the shore. We tried our hands at big game fishing, had a birthday party for David May at an impossibly expensive hotel, and spent two super days with his sister who had a villa out there. What a paradise, and it was with a sharp bump that I came back to earth, remembered who I was, and sent up a message of thanks for this memorable interlude, so far in many ways from the Itchen Ferry.

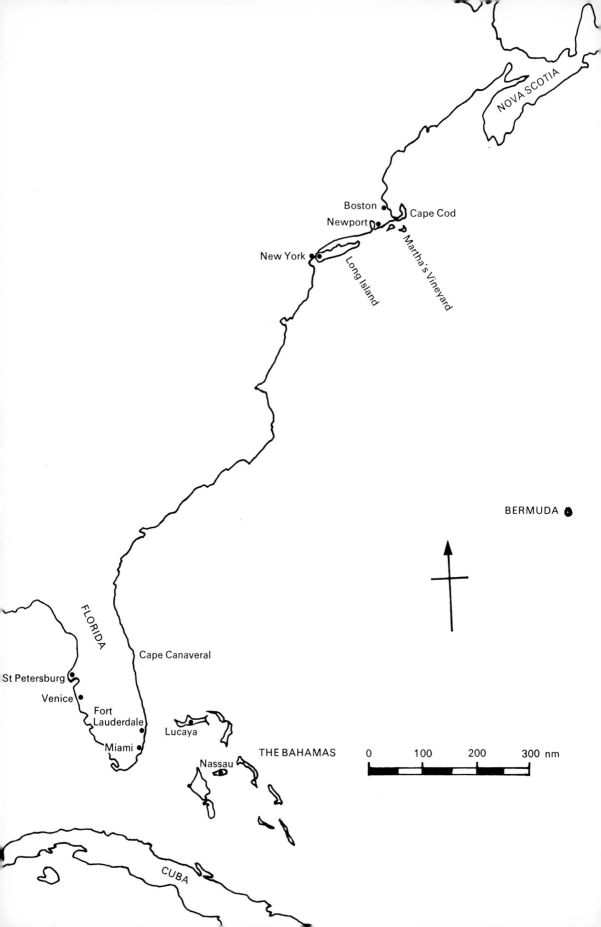

NOVA SCOTIA

Boston
Cape Cod
Newport
Martha's Vineyard
New York
Long Island

BERMUDA

FLORIDA

Cape Canaveral

St Petersburg

Venice

Fort
Lauderdale
Lucaya
Miami

THE BAHAMAS

Nassau

| 0 | 100 | 200 | 300 nm |

CUBA

And so we come back to where I was born. I have to agree with Uffa Fox, who once said that the Solent is King, because no race there is ever lost until the finishing gun has been fired. The tides and currents are so infinitely variable that foreigners at first often refuse to believe them. Local knowledge is of prime importance, and more power to those Admiral's Cup teams who come over, explore the waters and test the currents, and then beat us at our own game without taking a local man aboard. There are some boats who feel it wise to ship a south coast crewman for the early races at least, and there is no doubt that they profit from it, but the top boats these days know the Solent nearly as well as we do, and sometimes the so-called local experts can lead to trouble by trying to be too clever, merely to prove their knowledge. Previous experience is all very well, provided the conditions are exactly the same, but it only needs one factor to be different and things can go badly wrong, and there are so many variables that this can happen all too often. Nevertheless it is a fact that, as a country, we have a big advantage in the Admiral's Cup through sailing in our home waters, and this is borne out by the number of times we have been successful in the series.

I sometimes wonder whether we would have been wise to take an Australian with us during the 1973 Southern Cross series–but then, would we have put any resulting success down to our own ability or the fact that we had been saved a lot of thinking? Would he, in fact, have given us good advice? There is no doubt that there is greater satisfaction to be gained from your own unaided efforts.

The tides in the Solent can make for both interesting or frustrating racing. The Round the Island race of some 65 miles offers a wonderful day's sailing to large and small boats alike–indeed, it is often a small boat's race. With something like 500 starters, there is a tankard for every finisher and it is looked upon by many as a family outing, with the added spice of being able to be sure of a local boat-for-boat battle wherever you are in the fleet. It has considerable prestige these days and the front end is hotly contested, with the heavy metal trying to save their time on Half-Ton Cup boats being sailed like dinghies. We have the unique record of winning overall three times in a row, the first two times in 1971 and 1972 in the second *Morning Cloud*, followed by the bigger *Cloud* in 1973. This gave Mr Heath a terrific amount of pleasure, for the race remains a festive occasion and he always enjoys this kind of event.

Burnham Week is another fixture in the same vein, and has always figured high in *Morning Cloud*'s engagements. We usually go to Ramsgate first, to sail in the waters which Mr Heath knows so well, and are disappointed if we don't do well in either the Round the Goodwins race or the Gold Cup. Then on to Burnham, with its social activity in a more limited company than the bustle and press of Cowes Week. We have a special affection for this rather late regatta, and here again we have set a record by winning all seven races out of seven; this was in the second year of the

Fig 27. Light weather
racing at Cowes in the
third *Cloud*. Left to right
in the cockpit Peter
Ramage (ex *Sunmaid*),
my son Terry, self,
Edward Heath and
Rennie, my brother.
*Photo: Daily Telegraph*

second *Morning Cloud*, after she was shipped from Australia following the Southern Cross series of 1971.

I'm a Solent man and, if I could only sail in one country, it would have to be England. But I'd as sure as hell miss the Australian scenery and competition, and the American hospitality and keenness; I'd hope to see the New Zealanders and the Germans over here, and all the other fine people I have met during my career. Fortunately the possibility is not likely to happen and I look forward to more years of international sailing with the friends I have made round the world.

## Morning Cloud Routine

It seems fitting that I should end this chapter on people and places with a look at the people I know best–in other words, how we run *Morning Cloud*. We have always worked the naval watch system of four hours on and four off, usually having dog watches to ensure that the same man does not find himself on deck at the same times of day throughout the race (did you know that the name 'dog' watch was derived from 'dodge': it was to see that the same duty was dodged). This is by no means an invariable rule because, if we are all happy the way things are going on a short race, then we leave it that way. We don't shorten the watches in heavy weather unless it is also very cold, though we do switch helmsmen frequently under these circumstances. We don't have a set time on the wheel, largely because we have always been lucky enough to have plenty of helmsmen in the crew. If anyone is steering and he is obviously not doing too well, the watch leader or I usually suggest a change if Mr Heath doesn't mention it. We have never had to sit and fret as the helmsman makes a mess of things in any of the *Clouds*.

'I think you're a little tired, sir,' I say to Mr Heath, and he is always the first to agree to a change.

'Hey, Owen,' calls the watch leader, if it's me on the wheel. 'You're making a cock of it, let someone else have a go.'

Even the best helmsman gets tired offshore from time to time without realising it, but it becomes quickly evident to his mates. He may be getting his $7\frac{1}{2}$ knots, but he is sailing three or four degrees below the close hauled course; or he may be pinching, in an effort to point high; or else he is sailing too free in an unconscious attempt to keep a shy spinnaker drawing. No one is above reproach on board, but we never rub it in–not if the culprit doesn't try to argue.

About the most serious sin which can be committed is to fail to call for help on deck when it is needed. The man who is confident that he can do a job on his own can go ahead and do it, but woe betide him if he has to struggle when there are fit men below who could help him.

'I thought I'd let them sleep on,' is no excuse when a snarl-up occurs because there were not enough hands on deck.

NORTH SEA

Heligoland

Fastnet Rock

Burnham
London
Ramsgate

Southampton
Cowes • Nab Tower

CH1
• Cherbourg
Channel Isles
Le Havre
Deauville

0    50    100   150   200   250 nm

BAY OF BISCAY

Fig 28. The waters of
northern Europe,
showing some of the
places and turning marks
mentioned in various
chapters.

With a crew of ten we have Mr Heath and the navigator out of a watch, because they are liable to be called at any time. I usually try to be a floater as well, because I like to be on deck when anything is happening, and the Skipper likes to have me around when he is topsides, but I sometimes find myself as a watch leader. We thus have four in a watch, which ought to be enough for most jobs in reasonable weather, particularly now that twin groove forestays are standard; it was always a bit of a struggle to smother one genoa and hoist its replacement quickly with only one groove, so a headsail change used to call for all hands, specially when we only had six or eight in the crew, if we were not to be bald headed for too long.

It is in heavy weather that the watch below is most likely to be called out early, and we have lifelines and anchorage points by the hatch so that they can hook on before coming on deck. Mr Heath has provided everyone with oilskins which have a built-in harness and some buoyancy, so there is no excuse for failing to wear a safety line; the Skipper is specially particular about this sort of security measure in heavy weather and at night. I'm not saying that a ten knot breeze and a calm moonlit night will always see me wearing a harness, but as soon as it gets really dark or lumpy, on it goes, especially if I have to go on the foredeck, and this is the rule for everyone. We also carry spares for any non-regular crew who may be along.

As I said earlier, the first boat had a well equipped galley with all the different sized plates and bowls, even cups and saucers. Now we are down to three saucepans, and each man has a deep sided plate and a very large mug. A mug can hold much more than coffee or soup, and we find that it is first class for scrambled eggs, sausages and beans, stew, or pretty well anything except perhaps steak or eggs and bacon. It will not easily spill, it holds a lot of food, and it has a handle so that it can be held when hot or hung up safely when not in use. We always eat off our knees (there's not much else you can do if you don't have a table), each man dipping into his mug or juggling with his deep plate.

As a large proportion of overnight races start on a Friday evening, we try to feed and clear away the meal before the race. This leaves us with breakfast the next day, which is usually scrambled eggs, perhaps with a tin of tomatoes, toast and mar-malade, and coffee or tea. Then we have a fairly light lunch, maybe a cold chop or cold sausages with bread and butter. The main meal of the day is supper, which the watch below prepares and eats, before going on deck to relieve the others, who come down to their meal already cooked or heated, and their job is to clear up and wash the dishes. Steaks are excellent when racing, because they are easy to cook and to eat—they can be put between a couple of slices of bread if the weather is too rough for plates. We also go in a lot for stews, which are easily dealt with in our big mugs. During a race we always have a tuck box going, so that those who are hungry can eat between meals if they want to (and you use up a lot

of energy, so this happens quite a lot). There are Mars chocolate bars, Kit-Kat chocolate wafers, apples, biscuits and, of course, the perennial cup of tea or coffee, with meat extract drinks such as Oxo or Bovril for variety.

We have been lucky over seasickness. I have never been sick at sea in my life, and seem to be blessed with what is known as a cast iron stomach; some of the crew have resorted to various remedies from time to time, and modern pills are extremely effective when you find the one that suits you. Mr Heath has a stomach as reliable as mine, and I have never seen him turn a hair. Even on the Sydney–Hobart when we were bailing nonstop in very rough weather, head down in the bilges in a stench of leaking diesel oil, he kept at it for hours on end without even going pale–which is more than I can say for some of us.

## Social

Early in my association with *Morning Cloud*, I had a discussion with the Skipper about the amount of time which crew members have to spend away from home if they are to be regulars; this demands sacrifices from wives and girl friends. Mr Heath was quick to see the importance of this and on several occasions has included the crew's better halves in social functions. Later, when he was Prime Minister we all went to Chequers more than once, with everything laid on including a swim in the pool. After being treated like queens and having the chance to be shown round the official country residence of Her Majesty's First Minister, which we all read about but few of us ever see, no wife or girl friend ever again complained about being a grass widow due to the *Cloud*.

Being with Mr Heath has, of course, led to a certain amount of limelight. There are often reporters about, and there have been fascinating radio and television appearances. When we came back from Australia the first time, we were all on the BBC Sportsnight TV programme from the London Boat Show in January 1970. All six of us crowded into the cockpit of an S&S 34, sister ship to the first *Morning Cloud*, and appeared all over Britain.

This sort of publicity is all very well while it is under control, but it can become tiresome at times, especially when press launches crowd in on you while racing; it also brings with it a certain responsibility. We have to be on our guard when ashore that we don't let the Skipper down. If any crew member of *Morning Cloud* gets out of line, he wouldn't get a second chance. We even have to watch how much we shout at other boats when racing, because a national figure naturally has to safeguard his image. I don't say that we never have a joke, but we accept this and, in fact, prefer it to the boisterous antics of some of our more extrovert colleagues. That's not only my opinion, for the crew have shown by their loyalty to the boat that this is their preference. We had George Stead from Southern Ocean Shipyard as relief helmsman for the 1971 Southern Cross series, and both he and Anthony Churchill returned for part of the 1977 season. Of our present crew, Terry Leahy has been with us since the third boat in 1973/4. He is a shipwright with Vosper Thornycroft and works in our boiler house, being the man who cranks the main coffeegrinder in the cockpit; he is also ship's bosun and a real tower of strength all round the boat in a hundred and one tasks. Both David Carne and Mark Dowland have been regulars for only one less season. David runs his own hydraulics business in Cornwall (we use his products in the *Cloud*), while Mark is a hotelier at Poole on the south coast; they both work the foredeck. With my son Terry and brother Rennie filling in when required, this forms the nucleus of the regular crew.

I have been asked more than once to compare the various *Sunmaids* with the *Morning Clouds*. It would take a hell of a good boat to match the atmosphere and friendship generated by Guy Bowles, but I think we have achieved it on several of the *Clouds*. Of course, we were 'gentlemen' in the *Sunmaid* days, out for a little gentle sailing, preferably in gentle winds. We did not have so many different sails to change as we do now and, even if we had, would probably not have changed them so often as we do now. There is much greater pressure to win these days.

About the limit of our extra exertions in *Sunmaid* was to harden up a bit if we were on a shy spinnaker run just before dark, then drop the chute and set the genoa; the hope was that our rivals would notice this and do the same, so that we could free off again as soon as it got dark and then reset the spinnaker. Or perhaps we would shout like hell on rounding a mark to get a right of way which might not be ours, or crank noisily at an empty winch and call 'Lee-oh' to try to convince the opposition that we were tacking. You don't get away with such childish tricks these days, and it is all down to solid grind.

Sometimes with only a couple of miles to go to the mark, I realise that we ought to change genoas. If it is a cold night and I am near the end of my watch, the temptation is to wait until we are round and have to set the spinnaker anyway. But then I think of the races which have been won and lost by seconds.

'You'll regret it when you are ashore later,' I mutter and force myself to do what I know is right. In the old days we would have left well alone, but I would have been secretly dissatisfied.

# nine  Boat for Boat

### The Tea-time Sailors

My fondness for the 6-metre may be old fashioned and nostalgic, but there was a magic to those boats. Usually crewed by three amateurs and two professionals, they were in fact small enough for one man to be capable of any task on board; added to this you could sail them single handed with ease. But it was the actual racing which gave the greatest fun, and the class did not deserve the rather patronising nickname of tea-time sailors given to all fixed keel dayboats by the offshore fleet.

The class in the Solent was a fairly hot one, equalled in Britain only by the Clyde fleet in Scotland. You needed a good boat and good sails, of course, but helmsmanship, tactics and sail trimming were all at a premium. The excitement of close combat, the thrust and parry of short tacking, and the surging speed of a spinnaker run made up a heady wine, which could be savoured again and again after the race; none of this was lessened by the fact that 6-metres were wet boats, so a lot of spray would fly about on windy days.

We professionals had what was in effect our own club among ourselves, for we used to gather together after racing in order to swap yarns, boast of our successes, or submit to the ribald jeers of our conquerors when we had made a mess of things. We were fiercely proud of our own particular owner and helmsman, but a bad day would sometimes stretch loyalty to its limits in the pub afterwards.

There is no doubt that boat for boat competition sharpens a crew in all aspects of their work, because you can see an immediate result when you get everything going properly. Racing neck and neck with a rival, the water rushing under the bow and the wind blowing salt spray in your face, you get a terrific kick out of a fine adjustment in the sail trim which gives you the five or six yards you need to reach the mark first. Equally, if you see an enemy creeping away from you, there is every inducement to examine your own boat minutely to find out why you are slipping back. The very equality of the top boats and their crews made for close finishes, and a race for the finishing line with two or three rivals overlapping produced some heart-stopping moments.

My introduction to this particular form of excitement was in the Dragon *Mehoopany* in 1945. I was 13 and still at school, but my brother Rennie was the professional on board so I got asked along when it was blowing hard, purely to act as ballast. This meant staying below under the cuddy at all times except when on the run, and I would help stop the spinnaker and listen to the characteristic slam...slam...of the rather flat bow as we pounded into the seas, and the gurgle of the water hustling past the hull just the other side of the thin planking. If ever I poked my head above the coaming, perhaps to see why a sudden remark had been made or to find out where we were, the result was always the same.

'Get your head down!'

So back I would have to go until we got on the run, when I was allowed up to look around and see how we were doing.

You might think that this was an odd way for a youngster to spend his afternoons, cooped up in a wooden box, sitting up to windward on the hard ribs of the hull with only a sailbag at best for comfort, and being ceaselessly pounded without knowing where we were. But it had always been my ambition to follow my father and brother, and be a professional yacht hand; so I couldn't wait until I was 14 years old and thus allowed by the law of the land to leave school and start earning my living. It's funny, but we say 'couldn't wait' and usually we mean 'had to wait impatiently'; in my case the phrase is literally true because, as we have seen, I started turning out part time for my brother's boat before that magic date.

As soon as I was 14, I started full time as we saw in chapter one. Summers were spent sailing, but we were usually laid off in the winter so had to find work in the docks or yacht yards. I worked in the docks as a rigger, and spent the winter months splicing and serving the wires and lines of lifeboats. This meant working in the rigging loft rather than outside among the boats, and I preferred it that way because I loved to listen to the older professionals yarning away in the relative quiet, and I learned quite a lot like that–soaked it in through the soles of my boots you might say. It was not until I was 18 or 19 that I moved into the docks themselves, and later still it was yacht yards, still as a rigger. You could earn good money there while waiting for the thrill of fitting out, which never failed to excite me.

But we have strayed from Dragon racing. I loved it, I loved the snatches of conversation as the crew discussed tactics and trim, the feel as the boat worked her way through the seas changing tacks as she went, the excitement and the whole atmosphere. Gradually, of course, I became useful, even if it was only to row off to fetch the owner from his club, but I also picked up a lot of sea lore and racing tips as salt water soaked into my veins.

From this part time amateur sailing in Dragons (I did not get paid; had they known it, I would cheerfully have given all my pocket money to be allowed aboard), I moved briefly into what they called the 'Q' class–in other words, 6-metres which were no longer young enough to be competitive with the latest boats. It is interesting to recall that, besides a fully active fleet of modern sixes, the Solent also supported quite a lot of their more elderly and slower sisters. The advantage for me was that I could see out better than before. Then I took a couple of deck hand jobs as explained in chapter one, before going to the 6-metre *Thistle* and three wonderful seasons with Mrs Dreyfus (I had the great pleasure of being in the same race as this boat as recently as 1978, and what a picture she made, still in racing trim and still with a professional hand aboard). We fitted out in the fourth year, but found ourselves the only local boat in commission, so the new 5.5-metre class gave the owner permission to use both her paid hands in *Sasha* (strictly speaking the rules only allowed one professional in 5.5's). We made the mistake of winning our first two races, so this concession was promptly withdrawn and, being the younger man, I found myself out of a job. Just like that.

My subsequent sailing with Mr Millar included a couple of seasons in his International One-Design. These boats were originally started about 1936, when it was realised that the 6-metres were getting pricey. They were a kind of one-design 6-metre with a cabin, intended to give the thrill of boat for boat racing without the attendant high cost. For instance their headsails were like the old No 1 jib of the 6-metre before Sven Salen introduced the overlapping jib at Genoa between the wars; similarly the spinnaker was a small one of fixed dimensions, the general idea being that a family could race the boat without a professional hand, although one was allowed (and usually carried). In addition the class was only permitted to buy new sails at certain intervals, and the cabin was arranged so that the boats would be usable for cruising–not that they ever were. They certainly provided a lot of fun, and a dozen boats were still racing regularly at Cowes into the seventies, as well as fleets in Norway and Bermuda. Once again, it was the combination of a truly one-design class and boat for boat racing which gave them their attraction.

## Olympics

I have never aspired to Olympic honours, partly because I am a big boat man and the cost is beyond my pocket, but also because of the rules regarding amateur status. These are ostensibly stricter than those laid down by the IYRU for all other racing, and I don't believe that I would ever qualify–once a pro, always a pro. I say 'ostensibly' because a certain amount of rule bending goes on, whereby some countries underwrite a good helmsman's lifestyle (perhaps by giving him protracted leave from one of the armed services) to the point where he lives for nothing, his boat is a permanent loan and his expenses are subsidised. He is not actually paid for sailing, which is the letter of the law, but he is more a professional than a yachting journalist or a sailmaker.

I don't say that I would not have been both honoured and gripped by the whole Olympic atmosphere if chance had come my way, but my path lay elsewhere, and my only near contact with Olympic sailing was in 1972 when Mr Heath was in Germany and had arranged to take the German Chancellor out to see a day's racing at Kiel. I sailed *Morning Cloud* over to Kiel and was duly on hand when the Skipper came down the night before, ready for the visit. News suddenly came through of the massacre of the Israeli athletes at Munich, and the next day's racing was cancelled. Naturally Herr Willy Brandt had other matters to occupy him and our trip was called off, so *Morning Cloud* was sent home.

I am not one of those who says that the whole five ring circus has reached the stage where it should fold up its tent and fade into oblivion for another two thousand years. Anything which promotes yacht racing at the highest level is to be encouraged, and the Olympic games certainly funnel money into the sport, even if it is never enough. Facilities are built, crews given the spur of competition, gear is improved and people travel the world. Even if a bit of needle creeps in, it can't be all bad while that is happening.

## Match Racing

This is a restricted form of 'tea-time' sailing, which involves two boats only, winner take all. In the nineteenth century, when yacht racing first started in earnest, there used to be a lot of match racing; rich men would wager hundreds of guineas on the ability of their boat to beat any challenger. This usually ignored any difference in size, so handicapping did not come into it. When the *America* came over to England back in 1851, she issued challenges of this nature to all and sundry, finishing up with the gauntlet being thrown down to all comers for a race round the Isle of Wight, a distance of some 65 miles. Thus started the saga of the America's Cup, and it is interesting to note that the small cutter *Aurora* finished under twenty minutes behind the *America*, despite being 47 tons as opposed to the famous schooner's 140 tons; there is no doubt that any form of handicapping would have given the smaller boat the race. But think of the drama and excitement we would have missed if England had won what, strictly speaking, is called the Hundred Guinea Cup–at least, that is what is written on it. I know, because I've seen it.

I cannot say that I look back on my time in *Kurrewa* for the 1964 challenge with any relish. In fact, it remains the unhappiest period of my racing life. This was not because I don't get on with 12-metres, or because we lost but, let me set the record down fairly, there was a clash of personalities on board–it was not just me, a number of the crew were involved. Anyway, that's all water under the bridge and it is good to have sampled the legendary 12-metre. They are fine boats, and we had some good duels with *Sovereign* as we battled for the honour of challenging. Certainly we perfected a lot of new gear, and equally certainly we were better crewmen as a result of the close and frequent competition. But the atmosphere was not quite right, and I was glad when it was all over.

Much more fun is the Royal Lymington Cup, originally the Congressional Cup in imitation of the American series. This is the

British match racing championship, and is staged at Lymington on the western end of the Solent. Helmsmen are invited to compete in a series of match races staged in half a dozen one-design boats, which have so far always been the same 32 foot cabin keelboat, the Contessa 32, a lively and well finished cruiser/racer produced by local builders J C Rogers Ltd. It is due very largely to Bill Green, who works with Jeremy Rogers, that British match racing got off to such a good start. He saw to it that J C Rogers not only organised the right number of boats, but provided yard facilities, personal encouragement, administration and general publicity in the right circles. The competition is now nearly as well known as the original American Congressional Cup (though the latter is contested in bigger boats), and it has been the means of giving British helmsmen the chance to sail against top skippers from all over the world, as they battle it out boat for boat in the smart little 32 footers. It is interesting to note that the French have been so taken with the idea that they now run their own equivalent competition.

You can judge the popularity of the Contessa when you realise that over 50 boats come to the line for Cowes Week racing, and that this number increases by about ten each year. I went to the Congressional Cup, as it was still called then, largely on account of Mr Heath as it happens. The event is by invitation only and he was asked to go in for it on the first occasion it was held. Unfortunately he could not spare the time, so the committee were kind enough to ask me instead. Each helmsman takes along his own crew of three or four, and they race against every other competitor in boats which are drawn for (the owner races aboard his own boat each time). A series of shortish match races is held, boats racing in pairs one against the other, with an agreed limitation on the number and size of sails which may be used. The atmosphere of the private duel which prevails in match racing is offset by the knowledge that the others are ahead of you or will be coming along behind in further pairs of boats, so you don't feel too isolated. Once again you get the thrill of close competition in evenly matched boats, where the slightest slip can cost you the race. I don't rate myself among the best helmsmen, though I'm getting better these days as a result of steering *Morning Cloud* quite a lot when Mr Heath can't get away, but I managed to break even by winning four out of my eight races (isn't it funny that it is only second thoughts which make you realise that this could have been put just as accurately by saying '...by losing four out of my eight races'? But it is winning which counts, not losing, and that is how I prefer to remember it). They have broadened the interest a bit more these days, by always trying to have at least one representative from each type of sailing: offshore, day keelboats, dinghies, the trade, the true amateur, the press and so on. It is certainly a competition which has caught the imagination of the various racing fleets, and it is a rare honour to be invited to compete, let alone to win the series. It is also extremely interesting to see how the dinghy helmsmen cope with the complexities of bigger boats; their skill at feeling their way to windward usually ensures that they finish well up the placings.

## Level Rating

As more and more people moved from Dragons and 5.5's into the offshore fleet, so they increased the pressure for boat for boat racing to be introduced to the handicap classes. Once you have tasted the thrill of struggling for that yard which you know will not only give you the gun, but will also make all the difference between winning and losing, you don't want to lose it for ever. With the best will in the world, a boat on her own in the middle of hundreds of square miles of water will never be as keyed up as when a rival is thrashing along beside her. In handicap races, we all know how we seize on another yacht near by which seems to be sailing at about our own speed, and it then becomes a matter of pride to beat her over the line. The fact that you have to give her time, or that she has a higher handicap than you, makes no difference; the fact that line honours, class winner or overall victory will go to somebody else, makes no difference; the fact that you two are, in fact, battling it out to avoid last place, makes no difference. It is the act of beating the other guy over the line which counts.

I must not leave you with the impression that the handicap fleet pounds round the course, out of sight of anybody else, and trying to reach the peak without the incentive of close competition. We race against the clock, watching the man ahead or astern all the time, and clocking his every move. We know to the second how much we can give away or expect to receive from our closest rivals, and the urge not to lose time by sloppy drill or lack of effort is riding with us all the time. But we still like to get our nose ahead, handicap or no handicap. And so eventually we got recognition of this strong desire. Somebody found the old One-Ton Cup, which had originally been sailed for in boats with keels weighing one ton, and had the imagination to put it up for competition among handicap boats of a certain maximum rating, but all racing level. You could therefore enter a low rated boat if you wished, but it would do you no good because the chap with the boat on or about the maximum rating to which you all had to sail would usually have a faster boat.

I was lucky enough to go in for this cup twice. The first time was just after the competition had been inaugurated. I had raced with Guy Bowles on the weekend rally to Yarmouth in the Isle of Wight one day in 1966. *Clarionet* and *Roundabout*, two brand new One-Ton Cup contenders, were also in the race and beat us all ends up.

'Don't bother to wrap her up,' said Mr Bowles, when we met Derek Boyer of *Clarionet* over drinks afterwards. 'I'll take her as she is.'

That winter we had a One-Tonner built and, to cut a long story

short, we went in for the cup at Le Havre next year. This was my
first experience of racing offshore and being still able to enjoy the
thrills of 'sudden death', when last man over the line gets no
attention at all. Already the big names were interested, Dick
Carter, Beilken, Paul Elvström were all there, and I remember
being just behind Rod Stephens in one race as we ran down wind,
he with a small staysail under his spinnaker while we had our light
genoa under ours (it was the first year we had ever had more than
one genoa in any *Sunmaid*). It was interesting to compare the
efficiency of his spinnaker staysail with our genoa as secondary
sails; we seemed to be slightly faster, but we never managed to
break through his wind shadow on that run.

We won the first race but failed to do anything in the second. The
third, and longer, race took us round CH 1 buoy off Cherbourg, and
we were fetching it nicely out in front as dusk fell and the wind
dropped. We watched two French boats making a bit of a mess of
things as they sank away to leeward against the beginnings of a
foul tide into the bay. We were all right and could just lay the mark
by staying hard on the wind: it was an object lesson in the value of
getting the tide on the lee bow, but we were making no way over
the ground, so we kedged. At dawn we were still anchored about
fifteen miles short of CH 1 and waiting for the tide to turn in our
favour; right down to leeward we could just see the two
Frenchmen, out of it. Or so we thought, until we noticed them
creeping along the shore followed by a small fleet of others who
had similarly not been blinded by the need to lee-bow the tide, and
then luffing out to round the mark before we had gone a painful
hundred yards on the making breeze. It was more than stupid not
to have covered them, it was plain criminal in the face of such
obvious local knowledge, and we deserved to lose. Coming from
the Solent with its tricky tidal streams, I should certainly have
known better; the Germans weren't fooled, for they won the cup
with *Optimist*.

Next year, therefore, it was Heligoland for the same competition, and I joined Mike Winfield in *Morningtown*. I really
enjoyed not having to bother about tides for a change, partly
because more now depended on your own skill and resource. We
found quite a lot of sailmakers and Olympic helmsmen in the fleet,
and I have noticed more and more sailmakers figuring in the prize
lists as the years pass by–a sure sign of the importance of really
knowing about your motive power.

Heligoland has a kind of primitive grandeur. The yacht harbour
lies low, surrounded by rugged hills (there were 200 steps up to our
hotel, as I vividly recall), and there were still plenty of bleak
reminders of World War II in the shape of the remains of U-boat
pens–for this was one of the main bases of the German submarine
fleet. Nowadays there is nude bathing from one of the beaches on
the sheltered side of the island, and it was interesting to note how
the boats would sail round that way on the days when there was no
racing.

There were certainly many nationalities present at this competition, showing that the world is the small place which so many people say it is. But rising costs are gradually limiting the number of owners who can afford to compete in this sort of event these days, though sponsorship is one way of ensuring continuity of expensive racing.

An indication of the popularity of this kind of racing is how the Ton Cup idea has spread. When the One-Ton Cup was first introduced in its present form, John Illingworth, that arch priest of offshore racing, wrote that he foresaw the day when there would be a Half-Ton, a Two-Ton and even perhaps a Quarter-Ton Cup; we now have all these and several more besides, so the Grand Old Man was as right as ever.

## One-Design Offshore Racers

The final logical step in this promotion of boat for boat racing in the cruiser/racers is to introduce one-design boats offshore, and this is on its way. It might not please the naval architects, who will not have so many one-offs to design, but it has surely come to stay.

One-designs have so much to recommend them that it is surprising that they have been so long reaching the offshore fleet. Apart from doing away with the need to ship boats across the world to contest a series (it cost £5000 to take four boats to Australia for the 1969 Southern Cross series; it is nearer £100,000 these days and rising all the time), because crews can fly out and take over boats lent to them by the host club, with the knowledge that they will be in craft which are basically just as good or bad as the rest of the competitors. Of course there will be differences, but you can't have everything. The boats themselves should hold their value well because if you don't have to go in for all the latest rule cheating devices, you can select a seaworthy design which will last for twenty years or more. What is more, if she is well fitted out, simple and not an extreme shape, she will probably be less temperamental and thus more acceptable to the purely cruising man, so ensuring a better secondhand market than some of the stripped out racing machines we see today.

So here's hoping that those responsible for selecting designs will not be tempted by the latest tricks to achieve a good rating. If they do, the boat will only rate well for one or two years, until new ideas arrive to outdate her, but she will surely be less seakindly than she might have been. And if all boats are the same, surely it is more important that they should be strongly built with, for instance, a good run of keel so that they can take the ground on piles (and be less likely to broach than their more racey sisters with little more than fixed dagger plates), and proper bunks, galley and toilet facilities.

The opportunity is there, and I hope it is properly appreciated and grasped.

# ten   The Sailing Master

Those of you who have got this far without giving up may be wondering when Parker is going to start laying down the law about what makes a good sailing master. Now, I'm an easy going chap who doesn't like too many rules and regulations, as some of you may have noticed. Except, that is, where sailing is concerned, because sailing is too good to be taken lightly. So let's look at this business of being professionally involved in one's hobby.

First and foremost, it might be worth setting down the various headings which I think are important. Then we can examine each in turn.

What is a sailing master?
The boat
The owner
The crew
Tactics
Personal qualities
Going abroad
Absence of the owner

## What is a Sailing Master?

The first thing a sailing master must remember is that the owner pays the bills, and is therefore entitled to the final say in everything concerning the conduct of the boat. Having said that, it would be a peculiar owner who decided to have a sailing master and then withheld his confidence, because this very decision should bring with it a large degree of delegation–of confidence, in fact. When is the boat to be slipped for a scrub, which races may safely be left out of the calendar, which crew will be the best for a specific series, can such-and-such a sail be spared for a couple of weeks while the sailmaker breathes new life into it (can, indeed, that new life be given it or should the sail be replaced), will the watch system be all right for this particular race, or should the skipper tack now or perhaps give up the helm to someone else?

These and a thousand others are typical of the problems which confront the average sailing master throughout the season. Often an owner will wish to reserve for himself some of these decisions– he may prefer to decide his own race programme even if he cannot be aboard all the time himself, or who shall make up the crew, but

it would be an unwise man who ignored expert advice on important points. I have already mentioned how we always put a lot of these things to the vote in *Morning Cloud*, but there are some where Mr Heath sounds the various views and then decides which one to adopt, others where he consults my opinion before making up his mind, yet others where he leaves it to me to get on with it, and some where he will decide on his own. The sailing master is really the owner's representative, and should be prepared to act in his best interests in all matters concerning the boat.

## The Boat

The boat starts to take shape long before she is built. There are discussions in which the whole crew take part, each voicing his ideas on how his particular specialist function will be affected by the design. The owner then gets together with the naval architect of his choice (I am assuming a one-off design) to thrash out the general concept–the selection of a naval architect is often the result of considerable discussion on its own. The sailing master should be at these early meetings with a list of points already decided; he should also be there at the later stages, where the detailed layout of deck and accommodation is planned, once the general hull shape and weight have been settled.

Frequent visits to the builder are important while the boat is taking shape. If the owner cannot get down regularly (but there are not many who cannot spare the time to watch their creation taking shape–if he is not able to get away while she is building, be prepared to find that he won't find time to race her once she is in the water), then the sailing master has an even greater responsibility to liaise with the yard, and this hots up as progress is made.

Of course, none of this is necessary if the boat already exists, either as a secondhand purchase or as a standard production job. But even then, minor modifications can be incorporated in order to adapt the layout to established crew drill, or else the drill must be changed if it does not fit into a layout which cannot be altered.

Once the boat is in the water and ready for racing (or cruising), the sailing master has a number of tasks which may seem dull and routine, but which have to be done. Often the owner of a Class I ocean racer is a busy man (earning the money to pay for the luxury of tearing about the water at all of 10 mph), and the detailed administration of his boat is something which he has to leave to somebody else. If there is no suitable personal assistant or secretary in his office to whom he can delegate these chores, then they fall to the sailing master. Does she need a scrub? Can the engine be attended to before Saturday? Are the water tanks full? What about fuel, food, sails, new jib sheets? And so on.

As I say, this may sound routine, but you get fond of a boat no matter how many you have known. Sometimes you long for one which has served you well in the past and is long since in other hands, but it's the one you have now which is the important factor in your life, and you treat her like the lady she is. Like most women, she can be fickle, even capricious, but she will nearly always respond to loving attention. We can take the analogy further and say that some like being squeezed and pinched, while others protest immediately and prefer to be coaxed gently. They are all expensive.

## The Owner

It goes without saying that the owner and the sailing master should get on well together. If they don't, then they should dissolve their association and seek other partners. For that is what is involved: a partnership of mutual trust and respect.

### John Millar

I shall always be grateful to John Millar for introducing me to the business of yacht fittings. He was a good business man, and it was he who showed me the world of commerce and that there could be more to life than sailing as a professional. So I started to think about my future in terms of money and not just sailing, thus setting my feet on the path which has brought me where I am today. I also learned early in life to keep my eyes open in matters of business, and the importance of being first in the field with new products.

Mr Millar was a good helmsman, without being entirely dedicated. He could have a good time sailing without having to win, and this was in the spirit of the times. My cousin Mike Newton used to sail with us in those days, so he had some of his early training there as well, before becoming paid skipper for Mr Owen Aisher.

### Guy Bowles

I have always looked up to Guy Bowles for his unfailing courtesy and great ability as a helmsman; he trusted and respected my experience and judgement in all sailing matters. It was Mr Bowles who opened up a new life for me when he invited me into his social life as an equal while sailing. This may sound insignificant, but in those days a professional was kept very much in his place and it was a big step to take. His friends probably raised their eyebrows to start with, but they soon got used to it. I took a little longer, but my gratitude has lasted longer still and it is Guy Bowles who holds the warmest place in my heart among my sailing friends.

Nowadays I know which knife and fork to use and I don't actually foul the carpet, so I can be confidently taken anywhere. But the social world of the 1950's was a funny old place, because in my turn I was shocked at the behaviour of the upper crust once they had a few drinks inside them. In my circles down at the Itchen Ferry, we would never have taken off our coats when eating out, especially in mixed company. So each side had some adjustment to make. I remember watching with fascinated horror as he and his friends borrowed bicycles from a French café and proceeded to stage a medieval jousting match using long French loaves as lances. We semi-pros could not afford to let our hair down like that or we would never have been asked again; we had to be on our best behaviour and act the gentleman more than the gentry. I was never more aware of this than when I found to my surprise that the girl I was chatting up in one French bistro was the stripper–quite a shock in those days for a rather immature young man.

## Edward Heath

I respect Mr Heath for being a great gentleman in the finest sense of that word. He thinks of others, not as a conscious effort, but automatically all the time. When we won the Sydney–Hobart race, the telegrams of congratulations poured in–there must have been nearly two hundred of them. He read every one of them out loud to the crew, and personally answered them all. When the request to appear on Australian television was received, he realised that it would mean a good deal more to the crew than to him so he asked us to do it for him; the boys pushed me forward and, indeed, I shall never forget trying to answer intelligently the questions of the interviewer, while having to ignore the ribald gestures of the rest of the lads secure behind the camera.

Mr Heath is also a great leader, and it is right to say that the boat always goes better when he is on board. His presence lifts us, and he seems to know exactly how much to give us our heads and when to give us encouragement if we need it. On the final 24-hour beat to the finish at Hobart in 1969, conditions on board were very bad. We had water, diesel oil and cooking gas fumes swilling about down below, there was a force 7–8 blowing with attendant heavy swell and chop, and the six of us had been cooped up in a relatively small 34 footer for four days; sail bags seemed to be everywhere and we were all soaked to the skin and very cold. Mr Heath showed by example what should be done: he bailed, he steered, he encouraged and he bailed again. We could easily have lost enthusiasm in the welter of chaos, and gone on like zombies praying for it all to end. Instead, we rose to new heights and fairly drove that boat to the finishing line in spite of the appalling conditions.

He has evinced these same qualities again and again since then in lesser situations, and I like to think that he has come to have a respect for my own contribution. He has often shown this on occasions where a tactical decision has to be made quickly. He will start to discuss the various arguments for and against, realise that I want to get on with the job, and so will close the discussion abruptly.

'All right Owen,' he will say. 'Do what you want. Only do it quickly and don't hang about.' Then he may add with a grin. 'But you'd better be right.'

## The Crew

The reader will have noted from the chapter on the America's Cup that this was not the happiest period of my sailing career. I have to put part of the reason for our failure down to poor crew morale. There was no confidence between *Kurrewa*'s afterguard and foredeck, and I must take my share of the blame for this, because I was the link man between the two. Let me stress that the owner was super, but there was a relationship problem on board and the principle is the same whether it be owner or helmsman. It is not something I want to go into at any length, but it is an instance of lack of the mutual respect which I have tried to show is so important in running a happy ship. The fact that our helmsman not only flew out to America in a different aircraft from the rest of us, but lived in different quarters and often attended different social functions, didn't help towards close co-operation. It may be contrasted directly with Guy Bowles introducing his somewhat awkward ex-professional skipper to his own yacht clubs, and Mr Heath's invariable practice of always going everywhere with all his crew.

It is, of course, the owner's ultimate right and duty to choose his own crew. But the sailing master should have a broad enough knowledge of who should be tried out in which particular slot, and his advice on selection should be specific and firm. In *Sunmaid* it was Mr Bowles who chose the nucleus of his crew from among his own circle, but this had to be built on and expanded, and sometimes a member would drop out for one reason or another. I would then suggest a man and he nearly always fitted straight in. The competition in those days was not quite so hot and standards were not so high, so it is true to say that any competent sailor could hold his own provided he fitted in with the rest of the team. Even in the earlier days of the *Clouds*, you could get by with specialists who were rarely called upon to venture outside their own territory—helmsmen stayed in the cockpit, the navigator stuck to his charts and pencils, and the foredeck men were seldom employed aft of the mast.

Nowadays the competition has hotted up to the point where each man has to give up a lot of time and be able to fill several roles, so that the winch men can work the foredeck and steer a bit as well, the helmsmen need to be able to gybe the spinnaker under most conditions and take in a quick reef, and the owner has to know the finer points of trimming headsails. In *Morning Cloud* we usually try out people who have either been suggested to me or who I know already and think might be useful, and we try to have several possibilities under consideration whenever we need to make up numbers. The regular crew then passes judgement on how they think they will get along and I put to Mr Heath the names of those we all agree might be right for the team. If there is more than one suitable candidate, Mr Heath makes the final decision.

As I said above, the modern crewman must be able to turn his hand to many tasks. Perhaps it is more true to say that the helmsman or navigator who only steers or navigates has had to learn more about the mechanics of crewing the boat than he needed to know in the 'sixties. Top class racing boats have moved from the unsophisticated stage needing only eye and judgement, to being complex items of technology which have to be tuned to a predetermined pitch and then operated almost like scientific instruments. Everyone must play his part in keeping the basic structure in peak condition, and it is important that any manoeuvre or sail change shall be possible without calling a specialist from the other end of the boat, and thus endangering the correct trim which has been so painstakingly established, perhaps over a period of ten minutes. It goes without saying that the sailing master should not expect skills which he does not himself possess to a fairly high level, or he will not carry the respect of the crew. In his turn, he must respect the skill of the navigator and the helmsman, each of whom can lose a race more quickly than anyone else but who have both to be consistently right if it is to be won.

This respect is important in another way. Before and after a race there are always plenty of chores to be done which are not popular. Decks have to be scrubbed, the cockpit cleaned, the accommodation swept out, order re-established in the galley, and sails sorted, to name but a few. Most of these are done automatically by a good crew, but I usually find that everyone wants to work on deck and no-one likes going below as soon as the boat is tied up. Equally, any excuse is welcomed if it shortens a job when the boys are tired. This is where the sailing master comes in; it is he who has to crack the whip and drive the gang when they least want it. We were tied up at the end of a race to France one day, and the lads were keen to get ashore, so that those hosing down the deck stopped when they got to the cockpit where Mr Heath and I were discussing the race. The water stopped flowing and slowly I realised that the hose was being coiled on the dockside.

'Hey!' I called, breaking off what I was saying to the Skipper. 'We can move, but that dirt won't unless *you* shift it. Bring the hose back and finish the job.'

They moaned, but in the ultimate they prefer it that way. No-one likes a slovenly ship or an undisciplined crew, least of all the crew itself. The proof is that they come back for more of the same medicine and we never have trouble finding a strong team. I have to take unpopular decisions at times, but they know it is always in the best interest of the boat.

## Tactics

Tactics involve the minute to minute handling of the boat in the presence of other competitors, and to take advantage of local currents or tidal streams, so as to get round the course before anyone else. This is different from race strategy, which is the

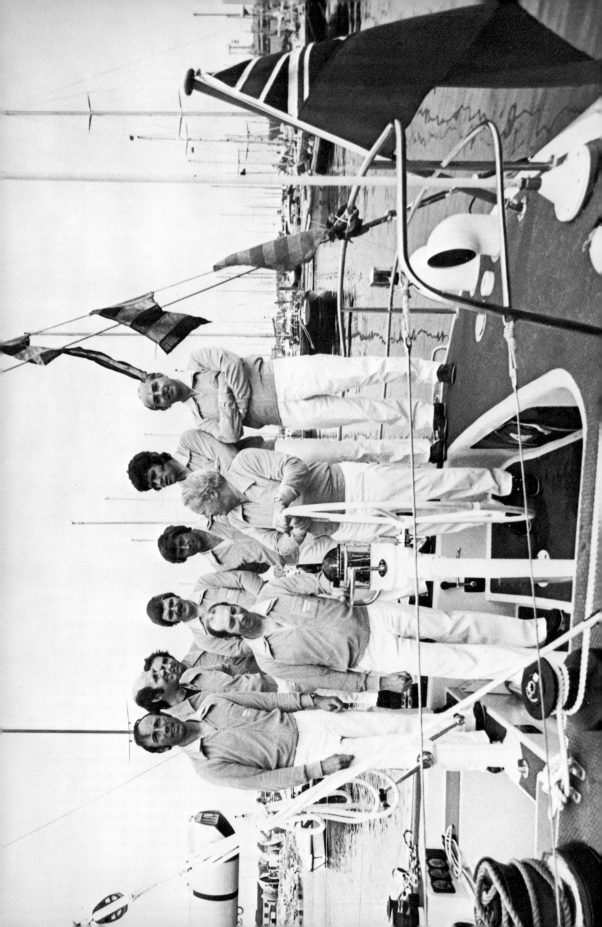

Fig 31. The crew
assembled around the
helmsman's cockpit of
the fourth *Morning
Cloud* just after
launching. Left to right
Duncan Kay, Ian
Godfrey, David Carne,
Mark Dowland, Richard
Halpin, self, Peter
Nicholson. In front Terry
Leahy and Edward
Heath.
*Photo: Sunday Express*

navigator's sphere and is partly decided before the start, but is also affected on long races by the weather.

The sailing master may or may not have a say in tactics–much depends on his own experience as a helmsman–so that sometimes the owner or navigator takes on this role, or a specialist tactician is included in the crew. In *Morning Cloud* I generally dictate tactics in my home waters of the Solent, as I know the area so well. This has now got me into the habit, and I am experienced enough to look after that side of things in other sailing grounds, unless we have someone on board who knows the area better–say a local owner at Burnham on the east coast. I also usually advise Mr Heath on the start, because this is a specialist skill and one which I enjoy. You need a particular kind of brain to get consistently good starts, so that one part of you can be assessing the future movements of other boats, while another part is counting down the seconds, and yet another is deciding the effect of your own actions. This all has to be done under considerable noise and pressure, and translated into unhurried orders so that you do not ask the impossible of the crew.

The tactician, therefore, needs to know fairly well the waters he is in, so that he can gauge the effect of the land on the wind (will it free or head the boat as the shore gets closer; will it die away completely under the cliffs or will there be enough to get over the tide?), and also have in his mind details of the tidal streams and any local back eddies. This basic information should lie in the background of his mind without conscious effort, so that the movements of other boats can be assessed and countered. To do this the tactician must know the areas of threat and disadvantage in the wind shadow round any boat on all points of sailing; he must also be able to think a couple of hundred yards ahead, seeing in his mind's eye the probable position of those boats nearest to him after a minute or two have passed. It is no good telling the helmsman to tack if, by so doing, you will put yourself into a position when you have to come about for the second time, where your opponent will be able to call for water on you or else sail you out into a stronger adverse current.

In *Morning Cloud* my extensive knowledge of the Solent means that there are few who question any tactical decisions I make when racing at Cowes. This is particularly true when you remember that the area is relatively narrow and usually congested, so that decisions often have to be rapid with little time for discussion. Mr Heath is usually happy to go along with any advice I give, without question; if he wants to argue about it, he will wait until the race is over and we then discuss it as a complete crew. I recall one occasion where I ordered up the No 1 genoa as we approached the leeward mark, only to change my mind after it had been brought on deck and the head fed into the forestay groove.

'No,' I called. 'Better make that the number 2, we could have 25 knots over the deck when we come on the wind.'

Then, as the No 2 was being pulled up through the hatch, I

changed my mind again, and called for the No 1 to be brought back. To make matters worse, time was now getting short and I had to get the lads to hustle it along.

'Sorry about the cock-up over the headsails,' I said when we were chatting over a cup of tea after it was all over. 'My fault.'

'Don't apologise, Owen,' replied the foredeck men who had humped the sails up and down the hatch. 'We'd have been put out if the decision had been the wrong one, but you got it right in the end, and that's the important bit.'

When we get out into the English Channel, or other open waters if we are racing abroad, there is often more time for discussion about tactical moves. We may then have a short seminar before I put the most favoured course of action to the Skipper, who then takes the decision.

A tactician should be able to think ahead, not only so that he can picture the situation into which he is putting his own boat in relation to the competition, but also so that he can give warning of his intentions to the crew. It is no good thinking up the most marvellous moves in what may be compared with an enormous chess board where every other piece is hostile, only to make a mess of crew drill because you forgot to say in advance what you wanted. This also goes for the helmsman. When I am conning the boat, say at a start in the Solent, while Mr Heath is on the wheel, I always try to explain what I think the others will do, what I want us to do, and how quickly it will all happen. This turns out to be a quiet, steady running commentary. At all costs it is important to be unhurried and in full control of the situation, even though the noise and clatter of gear and wind all round you is fighting to distract your attention.

'He's going for the line now, I reckon.' I will say. 'If we bear away as he goes past, tack and then come hard on the wind after about ten seconds, we should nicely cross that other chap and be just right . . . There he comes now, so bear away . . . Right. Tack now, Skipper!'

Of course, this all supposes that the tactician is more often right than wrong by a fairly hefty margin. If he is not, he will soon find his place being taken by someone else.

### Personal Qualities

Most of the personal qualities which I reckon are required of a sailing master will have become self evident from what I have written so far. You may be forgiven if you have conjured up some sort of superman in your mind's eye, because a story such as this is bound to highlight the successes. But we are all human, and the cock-ups occur, take my word for it, although I like to think that we have less than our share. These are, fortunately, becoming more rare as we all gain experience, for none of us ever stops learning.

This brings me to the main attributes I would list if asked to summarise briefly what makes a good sailing master. They are: experience, hard work, skill, and tact, with a certain amount of luck thrown in for good measure. Oh, I nearly forgot–you have to love sailing.

## Experience

It is no good trying to run a boat, be she racer or cruiser, unless you can command respect through the sailing experience you have gained over the years. It is, of course, no good having plenty of experience unless you have the common sense to learn from it, so that you are not caught aback by any situation. One of the first things to learn is that, as I have just said, you go on learning all the time you are sailing. I know that better men than I have said this many times before, but that is for the simple reason that it is so true; the sea is a hard taskmaster and should never be under-estimated. If you can respect the elements and recognise man's limitations, the enjoyment to be had from sailing is almost boundless. But treat him lightly, and Father Neptune will quickly bring you down to size.

## Hard Work

A regular life at sea has always entailed a certain amount of hard work, which reached its peak perhaps in the days of the big square riggers. Besides massive gear and primitive equipment, the crews of those days had also to contend with poor living conditions and harsh discipline. But the work of the sailing master is not all racing and winning or losing, and there is hard graft involved as well. I don't only mean scrubbing out the bilges if diesel fuel has leaked, or reeving a new halyard at the masthead in the freezing cold (though these chores also have their place). You have to be prepared to give up evenings and weekends, often at short notice, to attend to routine administrative matters: the propeller may need inspecting when the boat comes out for a scrub, the crew list has to be typed out and circulated giving details of the next race, you sometimes have to arrange extra ports of call before a race so that crewmen can more conveniently join the ship (and then allow time to call back again afterwards to put the same men off, because that is where they will have left their cars), it may be necessary to visit the sailmaker or rigger, or perhaps the owner wants a meeting mid-week to make future plans. Your time is never entirely your own because, if an on-shore gale blows up, your thoughts will be with the boat–and so should you be if the anchorage is exposed.

## Skill

A sailing master should obviously live up to his name by being master of all the various sailing skills, and have at least one at which he excels. This means that he can con the boat in narrow waters, short handed if necessary, take the helm, trim the sheets, handle the spinnaker, reef, navigate, know the rules of the road, mend a sail, have the emergency procedures at his finger tips, and mix a decent drink; in fact, be a good seaman. Most of these attributes arrive as the years go by, but some people absorb them better than others, and some of them are more easily come by than others. I don't know that I will ever make a top class navigator if I live to be a hundred, and I am fairly ham-fisted with a sailmaker's palm and a cocktail shaker (although the results are adequate, as I seem to be able to restore new life in both cases). But I reckon to know a certain amount about spinnakers and sheet trimming in general, and seem to be picking up the finer points of helmsmanship–although I have to confess to being prone to excitability as we near the finish and are winning; the perfect helmsman should remain unruffled, but most people allow their nerves to show occasionally and I can't resist looking over my shoulder, snapping at the crew over silly points and generally fidgeting. Fortunately most of them know me by now and shrug it off, but I admit it might irritate some people. I certainly lay claim to a good basis of seamanship, regardless of whether I fidget.

## Tact

Now we come to tact. You need it in your dealings with the owner and crew alike. There will be times when you have to be firm and others when you have to swallow your pride. It is sometimes all too easy to take the convenient decision, but the temptation to seek popularity this way must be resisted–you will recognise the situation as soon as you ask yourself what is best for the boat, and it turns out to be not what everyone wants to do. The owner, as I have already said, is paying the bills and is thus obviously entitled to the final voice, but any sailing master worth his salt will probably have a good deal more experience (we're back to experience again) than his owner, so he must learn how to steer the important things his own way without getting anybody's back up. The truly tactful chap can get his ideas across so surreptitiously that the owner thinks that they are his own, and never realises that they have been quietly placed some time earlier. Not that it comes to this very often, because most owners who sail regularly are good seamen themselves, so there is seldom a serious conflict of opinion. I have been lucky in both Mr Bowles and Mr Heath regarding one problem which I know gives some crews a good deal of bother. Whenever either of them has started to steer badly, as like as not they would recognise it themselves; if they did not ask to be relieved from the helm, they were always quick to respond to a suggestion that they might be tired. This happens to us all, but too often cold and fatigue bring with them a dulling of the critical faculties, especially the ability to be self-critical, so that sometimes a boat loses ground unnecessarily because nobody dare suggest a change of helmsman. As I say, I have been lucky in the *Sunmaids* and the *Clouds* in this respect.

## Going Abroad

I have listed this as a separate heading, because going foreign brings a number of extra responsibilities to the sailing master which are sufficient to warrant special discussion. The owner may very well want to look after preparation of the ship's papers himself but, even if this is so, some owners may need reminding of the fact (whereupon it will likely be the sailing master who will have to collect the form from the Coast Guard to warn them of the impending trip). Charts are the navigator's province and he will know what he wants, but he may turn to the sailing master if he cannot get the latest pilotage book of the area.

'D'you mind nipping down to the local bookshop and picking up a copy of *North Brittany Pilot* old man?' he will telephone. 'They've never heard of it in this neck of the woods.'

The cook may need a conference of some kind to decide food quantities, and where and when they should be delivered (when he should be on hand to mark indelibly and stow every item so that he will know where to lay his hands on it). The sailing master is entirely responsible for the safe anchorage or berthing of the boat, so he must ensure that all the right mooring lines and fenders are on board–you can never have enough fenders in a foreign port so, if there is room, buy a couple of extra big ones or, better still, make up a board which will keep you off the quay wall.

Before assembly of the crew everybody will listen to the latest weather forecast, but few will take the trouble to write it down. You can bet your boots that the navigator will be delighted if a written forecast is handed to him as he comes aboard. Fuel and water are part of the sailing master's job, as much as sails, rigging, engine, radio and safety equipment. Finally, don't forget to see that the Coast Guard is, in fact, told of the departure–it's no good having their form all nicely filled in, only to be discovered in the chart table twelve hours out . . .

## Absence of the Owner

If the sailing master acts for the owner while the latter is aboard, how much more does he do this when the crew are on their own? This is a responsibility which is a most serious one, and therefore not to be lightly dismissed. First and foremost, the sailing master should know what risks the boat is insured against. Is there a clause covering absence of the owner? Are the cruising limits wide enough? Is racing covered? What about third party and personal liability? Is the insurance comprehensive and does it cover you for salvage?

Once satisfied that normal risks are adequately insured, the sailing master must treat his charge more carefully than if she were his own. We come back to the point I have made more than once–decisions must always be made in the light of what is best for the boat. Never forget that you have a great deal of money under your command, not to mention the lives of the crew. Equally, you have the owner's personal reputation in your keeping, because rash or boorish conduct ashore or afloat will be put down to the boat and, long afterwards, people will not remember that the owner was miles away at the time. So the sailing master should be even more strict than usual, setting and demanding high standards of crewing ability and personal conduct.

You don't want the owner reading headlines in the newspapers on Monday morning which refer to anything about his boat other than a resounding win.

# eleven The Future

It is often interesting if not informative to peer into the future in an attempt to see how things are going to move. I am not saying that my particular crystal ball is any clearer than anyone else's, but it has been given a good polish so let's see what it shows.

## Rig

An area where terrific changes have taken place recently is the rig. Offshore racers have started to play about with their masts, just as sailing dinghies have been doing for ages. Apart from bending the spar, the whole sailplan can be shifted so that the masthead moves as much as four or five feet; this alters the position of the centre of effort and thus affects the balance of the boat, so that weather helm can be virtually eliminated. At the same time, mast bend makes a full mainsail flatter and also helps remove weather helm when close hauled. The rule makers frown on adjustable stays both fore and aft but, if it makes a boat more seaworthy, they may have to compromise.

The slight danger here is that the boat can be made so easy on the rudder that the helmsman fails to recognise that she is over canvassed. With the rail under and water flying about, the time has come to reef, but the fact is not realised. This is where inclinometers come in useful, and on *Morning Cloud* we start thinking twice when the angle of heel reaches a steady 22–23 degrees. Incidentally, we also have one of those devices lined up to give fore and aft angle; it is not all that useful, for the boat is seldom steady long enough to read it properly, but there are times in calm conditions when the bow-down attitude can be checked. Modern boats are extremely sensitive to trim, and it will always pay to bear this in mind.

Because hulls surf or even plane more easily these days than older designs, very large full spinnakers will tend to become less popular. This helps control and visibility without loss of speed, and is a factor to increase the popularity of the $\frac{7}{8}$ths rig. We have also gone in for rather smaller storm spinnakers than in the past, largely because big ones heel the boat so much when the wind goes on the quarter.

### Hydraulics

To achieve this control over the rig, hydraulics are needed in a boat of any size in order to deal with the loadings, and the rule makers are watching with interest. It is their task to see that owners and designers do not evolve unseamanlike boats in their single-minded pursuit of extra speed. Clearly, shifting the mast through large angles is not particularly seamanlike in one respect though, if it gives a boat which is more easily handled, who is to say that it is wrong? Well, for a start, the man who has just lost his stick overboard because his designer went too light. Anyway, restrictions have been placed on where hydraulics may be introduced into the rigging but, while I am sure that it is right to curb the over-enthusiastic, I hope to see some flexibility allowed.

I may be wrong, but I don't see a useful function for hydraulics in runners. Once mast rake and bend have been decided, runners are only set up when there is enough wind and swell to cause the rig to slam, so they are best adjusted by eye to take the weight, rather than to put any more tension on the mast. Similarly there does not appear to be an application in the area of the spreaders–and I would think that any attempt to introduce adjustable spreaders would be frowned on by authority, and rightly so because a failure would endanger the mast, to put it mildly.

## Spars

We used to have only one set of spreaders, even on a fairly big mast, but the change to slimmer sections has caused a move back to the even older habit, used in the days of wooden spars, of three and even four sets of spreaders, coupled sometimes with jumper struts. I'm not sure that all this complication is a good thing, and don't believe that it will last. But the pendulum must be allowed to swing all the way before it starts on its return journey, so we may have these mini radar aerials with us for a while before common sense forces us back to simplicity and better seamanship–with any luck improvements in mast making technology will speed the process (though attempts to introduce carbon fibres have not been really successful as yet). Certainly the cruising man would be most unwise to follow his racing counterpart's lead in this respect, because the former has no need of the slim section with exaggerated bend characteristics, or the ability to alter his rake for that matter. And if we can say with any degree of certainty what it is we want in a deep water cruising boat, we can reckon that we have a pretty good yardstick for the racer to aim at as far as seakindliness is concerned. After all, one of the objects of the IOR is to discourage extremes which might prove unseaworthy; in fact it is to encourage the exact opposite.

## Gear

### Winches

The first item I must refer to when discussing gear has got to be winches, because my career has been so bound up with them–I almost said 'linked'. Winches underwent a period of terrific development in the 'seventies: linked systems, molehills, three speeds, automatic gear change, self tailers–it is hard to see where the next advance can lie. Most likely it will be a gradual improvement in present equipment and materials, as the more sophisticated winches become available to all through reduction in size and price. It is hard to see any application of hydraulics to winches, except perhaps to the ultra racing machine, because this would be prohibitively expensive; in any event we don't want to take the human element entirely out of yacht racing. Winches are powerful and quick enough not to need any mechanical assistance or, for instance, to be able to be shifted bodily backwards on their bases to take up the initial slack. Pedal operation may come.

*Steering*

Introduction of masts which are adjustable over a wide range has made steering so much easier, on all points of the wind, that many big boats are going back to a tiller. Down wind in a blow, a boat which is hard to control can be a bit of a handful and very hard work with a tiller, and this is often the reason for installing a wheel (as in the case of the second *Morning Cloud*). A second reason is often the fact that rudders are being placed on the transom more often, and this invites tiller steering, particularly if the rudder is deep as is the fashion these days. A tiller gives more positive action and enables the helmsman to feel the boat better when going to windward. But wheel steering systems have recently done away with two pulleys in their linkage, by taking the wires down at 45 degrees and then through angled pulleys direct to the rudder; this gives better feel. The day may come when one of the requirements of a design will be that the rudder stock shall be vertical and conveniently sited so that a wheel may be mounted direct to it. It has been done, and control was said to be positive and sensitive.

*Rope and Wire*

Carbon fibres have been tried in rope with little success, because the material failed under flexing load (where the rope lay regularly at the same spot over a sheave), but success will come, if not with carbon fibre, then with another form of reinforcement, and we shall be the better for it. In fact, modern braided line with a hard core is near to the ideal; so small is the stretch that Class I boats can now use it for spinnaker guys (except for the front 6–8 feet, where the spinnaker pole still clips over a wire). Because it is so much stronger, the diameter can be smaller for any given use, which in turn means that it renders through blocks more easily. Here is an area where the cruising man benefits immediately from racing technology.

*Instruments*

Like a lot of men brought up to sail by the feel of the tiller in my hand and the wind on my cheek, I was dead against sailing instruments to start with. I expect some of the early ship masters didn't take too kindly to the compass when it was first introduced, preferring to navigate by sun, stars and known landmarks. But as time went by I realised the great use which they could be. No longer did you have to coil and cast the lead line, or use a dipstick in shallow water; no longer did you have to trail a log line to get speed and distance.

We used a Kenyon speedlog in John Millar's IOD back in the 'sixties; I must say, we started by being hypnotised by it, so that we paid too much attention to keeping the needle at a good figure and not enough to sailing a proper course. Then came the 360 degree vane, a most useful instrument when running in heavy weather at night to avoid getting by the lee, and with it the close hauled indicator which is a good check on course when beating to windward at night. One of the best, yet cheapest, aids to windward steering is the telltale. We have them on pretty well every sail and fine trim is turned into child's play. They all have to be used as confirmation of the helmsman's own senses, because it is still feel and touch, coupled with an eye on the next wave, which works a boat properly to windward.

One further use for the 360 degree indicator is to enable the navigator to predict accurately where the wind will be once you are round the next mark. This is important, as it can tell you whether to be on port or starboard gybe or, coupled with the wind speed instrument, whether you will be able to carry a spinnaker at all and, if so, whether it should be flat, full, big or small.

Electronic instruments have become more sophisticated but, like anything else, demand will enable mass production to bring down the price, while at the same time cheaper systems are evolved, such as the masthead arrow with guideline pointers, and wind tallies on the sails. Probably the greatest strides have yet to be made in navigational computers but, since these are not normally allowed when racing, the impetus to perfect them is not there, so they may take a little longer to reach general use. Perhaps round the world racing may help them along a bit.

Siting of dials is important, because it is distracting for the helmsman if he has to look round the cockpit to find the information he wants. Instruments should therefore be positioned so that they can be scanned when the eyes are moving in the plane between the genoa luff and the waves which are approaching. We once sought to protect the rather delicate equipment and keep down windage by suggesting that they should be kept below the bridge deck. Rod Stephens talked us out of it, reminding us that they would not be used properly in that position and would thus be a waste of money.

The next instrument? How about an attitude indicator to give angle of heel and fore and aft trim, rather like the artificial horizon of an aircraft?

## Sails

Probably the biggest revolution in racing since the middle of this century has come through sails. From the somewhat stereotyped creations of the cotton era, improvements have come in materials, trim and cut.

### Materials

Cotton was a lovely material to handle (when it was dry!) and, indeed, to look at. In those days you had some influence over the final shape of your sails, because careless breaking in–stretching as it was called–would ruin the flow. The skipper or sailing master, therefore, made or marred the shape, but the bother and sweat of it all were tedious. The inventions of nylon and polyester (Terylene or Dacron) revolutionised the sailmaker's industry, and it is hard to see where further improvements can come from. My friends in the sailmaking world tell me that research continues, with the greatest effort going into weaving, as continual attempts are made to reduce unwanted stretch in the canvas. This is not to say that nobody is trying to evolve an entirely new material for sails, because they are. We have seen the abortive attempt to incorporate carbon fibres into the weave, which failed when subjected to constant flexing, much as it did with rope, but my guess is that some sort of reinforcement will eventually succeed, rather than the development of an entirely new cloth. Indeed, two-ply cloth has made a successful comeback and it is now possible to weave the two thicknesses in one process.

### Trim

Awareness of the importance of sail shape and the interrelation of various sails has heightened enormously over the past twenty years. Whereas we used to hoist the mainsail and genoa to their marks and leave them there all day, we now realise something of what is happening as the sails drive the boat through the water. A good sail trimmer has become almost vital to success, and examination of the way in which sails turn the energy of the wind into driving force will always repay the effort.

While I am a believer in having a sailmaker aboard, others have now picked up his thorough knowledge of the subject of airflow and his advice should no longer be weighted more heavily than that of other crew members with a leaning towards the subject; any super-specialist tends sometimes to be unable to see the wood for the trees. Thank goodness that intuitive guesswork sometimes still has a part to play. A sailmaker in the crew has the advantage, however, that you can usually get priority treatment from his loft!

*Cut*

This business of understanding sail drive has led to a chicken-and-egg situation. Either control of sail shape is easier because owners wanted to be able to vary the draft in both mainsails and headsails, or else owners now give a lot of attention to draft and twist because the controls are available. Which ever came first, winning boats spend a lot of time on trim, and the sailmaker cuts his sails accordingly. This attention to drive has led to the development of subsidiary sails such as the tallboy, big boy or blooper, mizzen spinnaker and the like, all of which are racing sails only; the cruising man long ago got the only extras he really has any use for: the mizzen staysail and twin running sails. Fashion plays a certain part in this particular game, and it is a bold man who sets out to predict fashion. All I can say is that evolution is fast and furious, but the basics remain the same. If I were to be forced into a forecast it would be that there might be some work to be done in variation of material in different parts of the same sail–and I don't exclude a deliberate introduction of a porous cloth in an attempt to alter airflow characteristics beneficially.

## Sponsorship

As you will have gathered, I'm all in favour of sponsorship in sailing. I could hardly be anything else after the way I have been virtually 'sponsored' by various private owners myself. Just think of the way different firms have enabled boats to race round the world, owners send their boats to other countries to compete in special races, young men and women to sail in Olympic selection trials, and the general support which has been forthcoming for sailing over a broad field. Does it matter what brand name is written on the racing marks?

As costs increase (and, it must be said, as yacht clubs elect younger men to their race committees), I reckon that sponsorship will increase. I don't see why a boat has to avoid being called by a sponsor's name or even why a trademark should not be displayed on her sails; after all, we are quite used to seeing brand names plastered all over racing cars and advertising slogans spread round sports grounds. I don't say that everybody would want to be associated with this kind of publicity, but they would have the right to decline. The smaller boats and dinghies may have to look to the Government for sponsorship, so that youngsters can continue to enjoy the sport. This help may take many forms other than direct cash. Clubs could be subsidised, as could repair facilities, accommodation at meetings, instructors at schools and even boat builders of certain classes. This could be done by cash payments or tax relief.

You might say that all this would spell the death knoll of privately financed sailing. But there would always be room for this, particularly when you remember the terrific number of regattas and races held every year–sponsors could not be found for more than a select few. I agree, you might find it hard to enter for a trans-Atlantic race with any real hope of success unless you had a sponsor, yet if you have the kind of private money which such a race entails, you will always be in there with a chance. No, take the money which is offered, I say, and let's go on sailing in the big races with big boats. They will fade away like the J-class unless we do.

## Design

I am not a naval architect, nor do I know what the rule makers will do in the future. So I neither know which characteristics will be discouraged nor what shapes will evolve as a result. All I can do is look at the changes which have taken place over the years and hope that we get good boats in the future. There is no doubt that the old fashioned slab sided straight stemmed cutters of Britain, with their enormously long booms, evolved from the old Thames tonnage rule; that the CCA produced some graceful and seaworthy boats in America, usually fairly beamy; that the RORC rule encouraged rather narrow and undercanvassed boats; and that the IOR has allowed some temperamental vessels to be designed. The hope for the future is that the rule will continue to put the brakes on speed at all costs, because this can be fatal offshore. The one-design offshore racer presents a wonderful opportunity to encourage seakindly vessels, which will be equally at home as blue water cruisers or as competitive racers in their own international series.

Safety measures, always important, will continue to receive ever closer attention as technology improves radio and pyrotechnic aids. The RORC recognises that existence on board of the correct aids is not enough, and their scrutineers check that crew members not only know where everything is, but that they are trained in how to use it all. This is an excellent feature before all races.

### Racing

While there is still money there will still be development, for there will always be those who want to see the frontiers advanced. This expenditure is by no means always selfish, because sometimes the spenders don't even get to use the equipment which they are financing. There is not a lot wrong with yachting as long as there are men like the Livingstone brothers, Owen Aisher, Vanderbilt and Baron Bich prepared to finance other people's sailing for an ideal.

Next year's racing machine may not always be like last year's, because much depends on the rule makers. But one thing is sure: the racing man will always be on the lookout for a loophole in the rule, and the governing body will always be keeping an eye open to see that any such loopholes do not lead to unsafe vessels.

Unfortunately I don't see any great improvement in the comfort down below in a racing boat. The accent will always be on functional working rather than creature comforts, and this is as it should be. But there is a welcome tendency towards having internal furniture which can be removed for racing and replaced for cruising. I am thinking here of the toilet, the galley, bunks and table. In this connection, among certain boats there is a one-upmanship in seeming to be rather spartan in the accommodation when in the presence of other crews. This is the we-don't-have-time-to-sleep-we're-always-making-her-go-faster syndrome. I don't have time for this attitude, on the grounds that any fool can be uncomfortable and it takes intelligence to avoid it at times. I am glad to report that we have decent bunks with proper pillows in *Morning Cloud*.

One-design offshore racing will expand like wildfire once owners get to grips with it. It presents a wonderful opportunity to bring down the cost of international racing through the existence of fleets of identical boats all over the world, and the boats themselves should be able to hold their secondhand value. There will be nothing to stop the dedicated competitor from stripping out all luxury gear which is surplus to the rule, but there will also be nothing to stop that same gear from being portable, so that it can always be put back. This will encourage more wives to get afloat, and the equipment will be developed to enable them to race more often in spite of their usually slighter physique: steering systems are already easier, winches more powerful and ropes softer, so we have made a start. This is a good thing, because it will enable more owners to look upon their boat as the family holiday, particularly if it can be made more comfortable by adding removable joinery.

## Cruising

My story has been largely concerned with racing, because that is the testing ground for new gear and designs which eventually filter their way through to the cruising fraternity; that is where the money for development lies. This emphasis on the competitive side of the sport may excuse you if you are surprised to learn that over ninety per cent of my company's business is with cruising boats. If I had to give up one or the other, purely commercial considerations would force me to renounce the racing part of our trade. This may sound heretical to the many friends I have made on the offshore circuit, but we could never live as a business on the relatively few racing boats. So perhaps it is fitting that I should end this book with the cruisers.

What can we see ahead for the sailor with time on his hands to explore the wonderful cruising grounds of the world? He will obviously continue to profit from the money poured into the industry by the rich men who want to win. After gear is evolved and perfected for the racing fleet, it usually becomes cheaper and more available to the cruising man. It is rather like private flying profiting from research into aviation triggered off by the unlimited spending of a major war. Not everything is suited to cruising, of course, but there is a lot that is. I don't see any lessening of this process in the future, and hopefully shore facilities will improve at the same time to better the lot of the man who likes his creature comforts.

The popularity of round the world and trans-ocean races will continue to encourage development of rugged gear well suited to the blue water man's requirements. In fact, even though they are few in number, boats built for this sort of racing owe more to the long distance cruiser than to the offshore fleet. A bad broach or pooping off Cape Horn or alone in the Atlantic is as disastrous for one as for the other, so the boat has to be built to avoid the problem if possible, or ride it out if it occurs. To coin an alliteration, sails, spars, skylights and scantlings have to be seaworthy. Self-tailing winches are a first class example of the needs of the single-handed globe trotter being met, and then being immediately made available to the family cruising man.

Already some world cruisers are using solar panels to provide energy for on-board use. These will surely become more efficient and will eventually replace the need to run the engine to top up batteries; this will enable refrigerators to become more common away from shore power lines, allow the use of electric showers throughout a voyage, and a more liberal use of electric light when away from port for weeks on end. Electronic navigation aids will get cheaper in terms of real money, to the point where there will be no excuse for getting lost as doppler or inertial navigational computer print-outs give position in latitude and longitude, within the reach of the average man's pocket. Like transistor radios and pocket calculators, if you sell enough of them the price must come down.

Hulls will get stronger, sails better, we shall hopefully continue to race and learn, and . . . books will continue to be written.

# Index